D0045136

Cooking as Fast as I Can

A Chef's Story of Family, Food, and Forgiveness

Cat Cora
with Karen Karbo

SCRIBNER

New York   London   Toronto   Sydney   New Delhi

SCRIBNER
An Imprint of Simon & Schuster, Inc.
1230 Avenue of the Americas
New York, NY 10020

Copyright © 2015 by Catherine Cora

All rights reserved, including the right to reproduce this book or portions thereof
in any form whatsoever. For information, address Scribner Subsidiary Rights Department,
1230 Avenue of the Americas, New York, NY 10020.

First Scribner hardcover edition September 2015

SCRIBNER and design are registered trademarks of The Gale Group, Inc.,
used under license by Simon & Schuster, Inc., the publisher of this work.

For information about special discounts for bulk purchases,
please contact Simon & Schuster Special Sales at 1-866-506-1949
or business@simonandschuster.com.

The Simon & Schuster Speakers Bureau can bring authors to your live event.
For more information or to book an event, contact the Simon & Schuster Speakers Bureau
at 1-866-248-3049 or visit our website at www.simonspeakers.com.

Interior design by Erich Hobbing

Manufactured in the United States of America

1   3   5   7   9   10   8   6   4   2

Library of Congress Cataloging-in-Publication Data is available.

ISBN 978-1-4767-6614-0
ISBN 978-1-4767-6616-4 (ebook)

To my extraordinary wife, Jennifer, our fearless leader:
Thank you for your patience over the years
as I have learned to trust again.
My love for you is infinite,
and I am forever grateful for your strength,
wisdom, courage, and grace.

To my Iron boys,
Zoran, Caje, Thatcher, and Nash,
for whom my love is endless:
You bring an abundance of riches to my life every day.
Dream with your eyes wide open and your souls free.

And to little Cathy Cora, my younger self:
Forgive sooner so you can live and love with abandon.
Be the best friend you can be to yourself.
And last, enjoy the journey;
I promise it turns out pretty sweet after all.

Forgiveness is the fragrance that the violet sheds on the heel that has crushed it.

—Mark Twain

Cooking as Fast as I Can

~ one ~

I spent the first week of my life at the Mississippi Children's Home, waiting to be adopted. My name then was Melanie. The word means dark in Greek, and referred to my brown hair, my deep brown eyes.

My birth mother was sixteen when she got pregnant with me. It was 1967. Whatever free-love thing was happening in other parts of the country in the late sixties, it was not happening in Greenwood, Mississippi. A girl who got knocked up there brought shame upon herself and her family.

When she began to show, my birth mother was sent to a home for unwed mothers on the outskirts of New Orleans, where the girls scrubbed the floors and toilets with toothbrushes, penance for believing boys who said it would be okay. She was the youngest mother-to-be in the home, and on the weekends she was thrilled to be invited to go into town with her older friends, young women in their early twenties, also inconveniently pregnant. They would leave her at a cafe with their purses while they went out and turned a few tricks.

The day she went into labor, my birth mother was sent to the hospital. All the rooms were full, so she was left on a gurney in the hallway. A midwife happened past and took pity on her and wrapped her in a blanket, the tradition at the time. First babies are notoriously slow to make an appearance—

1

not me. Less than a minute later my birth mother hollered, "The baby! The baby's on the bed." The nurse, a soft-spoken African American woman, cried, "Holy shit, that baby done flown out." Or so the story goes. But sure enough, there I was, between my mother's knees, still tied by my umbilical cord, screaming my head off. I wasn't waiting until my birth mother had been settled in her room, wasn't waiting for the doctor to arrive, wasn't waiting to be invited.

Two hours away, in Jackson, the state capital, Virginia Lee and Spiro Cora received a phone call from an adoption agency where they'd filed papers to adopt another child. They were an upstanding middle-class couple—she a nurse, he a teacher—who had already adopted a son, Michael, and were hoping for a daughter. "We have a baby girl for you," said the woman from the adoption agency.

A week later, the people who would become my parents picked me up at the Children's Home and changed my name to Catherine Anne.

⁓

My childhood was as perfect as could be.

We lived on Swan Lake Drive in Jackson, in a development of low-slung, single-story homes built around finger-shaped Swan Lake. Our little house was across the street from the waterfront homes; our backyard gave out into what seemed to be endless fairy-tale piney woods—a true wilderness. There my brothers and I built forts and cut down a Charlie Brown tree every Christmas, then dragged it through the backyard and into the living room. Mike was three years older than me, and Chris, born not long after my adoption was finalized, was only thirteen months younger.

I had my first kiss in these woods at the age of eight. She

was a small blond girl with a pixie haircut who was visiting her grandparents for the summer. One of us thought it would be a rad idea to experiment with kissing. Her soft mouth tasted of Aim toothpaste with a hint of Orange Crush soda and the Green Apple Jolly Rancher candies we'd sucked on earlier. It was definitely better than kissing second-grader Johnny Purvis.

My mom and dad both worked full-time, but if there were better-loved latchkey kids, I'd like to meet them. At 6:00 a.m., Mom would flip on my bedroom light and say, "Time to get up!" Despite her own hectic morning schedule, she always packed our lunches. Hot school lunches were too expensive, yet my parents made too much to qualify for assistance. Peanut butter and jelly, egg salad, and bologna were the sandwiches in rotation. Sometimes if she ran out of peanut butter and payday was too far away, she substituted mayonnaise and jelly, the thought of which grosses me out even now. In those days, no one in the Deep South—even a trained nurse—thought keeping a sandwich made with mayonnaise in a metal school locker for six hours was a bad idea. But my brothers and I were well acquainted with the stink it caused, and would toss those sandwiches into the garbage next to the bus stop. (It was six houses down, a distance my mom felt confident we could negotiate by ourselves.) Unless we were lucky enough to have a PB&J sandwich that day, we made do with a bag of Fritos, a Little Debbie Oatmeal Cream Sandwich, and an apple.

Our dad taught world history at Wingfield High School, and he came home every day around four thirty. This gave us a good ninety minutes every afternoon to get into trouble, because once he got home, he would keep an eye on us by planting himself in his La-Z-Boy recliner, in his undershirt

3

and slacks, reheating a cup of morning coffee and reading the paper until Mom got home. He didn't believe in interfering, but he wouldn't let us think we were unsupervised.

First thing after we got home, we'd dump our book bags onto the floor by the door. We either made ourselves a redneck grilled cheese—white bread topped with "green can" Parmesan melted in the toaster oven—or else we'd turn on the FryDaddy and make ourselves some french fries. I can't imagine letting unsupervised grade-school kids loose around hot cooking oil, but back then in Mississippi, kids were raised to take care of themselves.

Mike always had a dumb stunt or two up his sleeve. I displayed my adoration for him by being his willing partner in crime. Once he showed me the art of smoking grocery bags. We sat on the porch, and he ripped a brown paper grocery bag into neat strips, then rolled them into perfect, tight little "cigarettes." We lit up and I sucked on mine until I barfed all over the front porch.

A few years later, when I was about ten, he convinced me to try dipping snuff. He was already a confirmed Skoal dipper, and his suggestion tapped right into that part of my personality that believes if it's wrong, there's got to be a part of it that feels really right. I took his challenge and shoved some dip between my cheek and gums. I thought I was a tough titty until the trees started spinning. That was my first genuine buzz. It sure wouldn't be my last.

If the weather was fine, we often enjoyed a little water-skiing on the lake, off the back of Mike's flat-bottomed jon boat. The vessel was built for fishing and poking around the shallows, but we were undeterred. We were eager to perfect our stunts.

If we saw some mom standing on her back porch with her hands cupped around her mouth shouting some version

4

of "You Cora kids, get out of that boat and go on home," we knew her next step would be calling our mom and telling her, "Your damn kids were out there skiing and left a wake that washed up and soaked my backyard." So Mike would cut the engine immediately and we would float over and apologize—yes, ma'am, and no, ma'am—hoping the mom wouldn't make that call. Even though Mike went on to become a minor criminal and confidence man, he was polite as pie when it came to accepting a dressing-down from the neighbors.

Even though we were allowed to fend for ourselves for a few hours after school, in the summer my mom didn't feel comfortable leaving us alone for an entire day. In addition to her nursing job, she sometimes worked as a home aide, and she would drag us around on her rounds. We were told to stay in the car while she went in and checked on her patient. It was as hot as Hades in Mississippi in the summer. We rolled down all the windows and waited dutifully, but thought it would serve our mom right if while she was nursing someone else her children died of heatstroke.

Our favorite stop was Mr. George, a sweet old Greek guy who always offered us cookies. He made his own apricot wine, thick enough to stand a spoon up in, which our mom graciously accepted as her payment. When we came over, he invited us to pick figs as big as baseballs off the tree in his backyard. One of us would climb up, pick them, and gently toss them into the waiting hands of the two on the ground so as not to split or bruise them. We ate until we had stomachaches, the juice pouring out of the fleshy red center onto our chins.

⁓

I don't think I'd lose a bet that my parents were among the most liberal in all of Jackson. In the 1960s, while they were still footloose young marrieds, they rented a ground-floor apartment on a steep little street close to the stadium. My dad was pursuing his degree in history at Mississippi College, while my mom worked at Mississippi State Hospital, nursing supervisor of the Colored Male Service, dedicated to caring for the black male mental patients. Like all southerners, they enjoyed their get-togethers, and were among the only people in their set to invite African American friends to their parties. This was still intensely frowned upon in Mississippi; they had to sneak their black friends into the house in the dark of night, which itself was dangerous. To welcome them into their home was to risk having their house burned to the ground, or worse.

Thus, they got along with all our neighbors on Swan Lake Drive: the Southern Baptist evangelical family, the Yankee family, the black family, and across the street, the bachelors—Dalton and Millard—the gay family.

My mom was terribly fond of Dalton and Millard. She knew they were a gay couple, although she never said so outright. When Millard would try to offer her the occasional decorating tip—no one was less interested in decorating than Virginia Lee—he would beg her to listen, saying, "I'm the queen." She would scoff and say, "You most certainly are not. *I'm* the queen." Then he'd say, "No, honey, you really don't have any idea what you're talking about. I am the true queen of Swan Lake Drive."

In her capacity as psychiatric nurse who also taught and also picked up extra work as a home health nurse, my mom knew a number of people who had nowhere to go during the holidays, and come November 1 she'd roll up her sleeves and start issuing invitations. On Thanksgiving Day, every type of human you can imagine appeared on our doorstep. Taxis brought people who arrived in their Sunday best, their wheelchairs stowed in the trunk. Some folks came on foot, having been dropped off on the corner of Lakeshore Drive by a driver going in the same direction. We had every color, creed, and sexual orientation, in addition to a lot of garden-variety lunatics. "They all bleed red," my mother would say.

My dad was a smidge less tolerant. He was welcoming, but a traditionalist at heart. He had his limits. One year, our friend George, a schizophrenic with some other mental issues that required some delicate alchemy of medicating, lined all the kids up on the couch and entertained us with his impersonation of Erica Kane from the soap opera *All My Children*. I was completely transfixed. My dad was less enthused and the following year he kept a careful eye on George and his theatrics.

One of my best friends in the neighborhood was Helene Gregorich, three doors down. Her family came from the North, Ohio or somewhere, and was of some sort of Eastern European extraction. Her mom, Mrs. Gregorich, made the most excellent Hungarian goulash, and I used to hang around moon-eyed, hoping she would ask me to dinner. This was not an easy task, since she worked the graveyard shift at the GMC plant on the line assembling car parts. We had to tiptoe around after school until she woke up and started dinner.

The Gregoriches had an in-ground swimming pool, which made them seem incredibly glamorous and rich. In the merciless heat of summer, hanging around for Mrs. Gregorich's goulash would be replaced by hanging around hoping to be invited to go swimming. Their impressive affluence knew no bounds: Helene had the best Easter candy on the block. My mom splurged for hollow chocolate bunnies from Walgreens for my brothers and me, but the Gregorich children received enormous packages of rich chocolate from their European relatives.

Mr. Gregorich was the coach for the softball club I joined in fifth grade. I went on to play for seven years. Catcher and center field were my positions. I had good hand-eye coordination and an ability to hurl the ball at the perfect moment to make an out. I was tapped for the all-star team year after year. The trophies still sit on top of my dresser on Swan Lake Drive, gathering dust. But damn if I don't love showing them off to my kids when we come to visit.

⁓

Come the end of May every year, my dad would hook up his boat—a snazzy Larson Shark—to the back of the station wagon and we'd take off for the Pearl River. His favorite spot was Ratliff Ferry, off the Natchez Trace. We camped on Flag Island, a sandbar, actually, with beaches as beautiful and white as any you'd find in the Caribbean. We slept in a canvas tent big enough to fit the five of us and all our gear. In the mornings my parents would percolate some coffee over the campfire, and we'd sit and watch the alligators cruise past, the heat already thick and approaching unbearable. No kitchen I've ever slaved in was as hot as summer in Mississippi. After coffee, my parents would hop into the boat, and my dad would drive my mom back to her car so she could go to work; in the evenings he'd pick her up and bring her back to camp.

We kids spent the day swimming and water-skiing. I was as brown as a nut. My dad would sit in his lawn chair and read his Louis L'Amour and Jean Auel. For lunch, he would make us bologna sandwiches, served with a handful of Lay's chips. Some years the cicadas would have emerged earlier in the season, and we would entertain ourselves picking their skeletons out of low-hanging branches.

At night, like dummies, my brothers and I would grab a

flashlight, hop into Mike's old jon boat, and cruise across the river to what we called "alligator swamp." Summer is alligator mating season, and our goal was to catch them in the act. We never got far; two sets of red eyes glaring at us in the dark were enough to send us scuttling back to our camp.

⁓

My childhood was as perfect as could be, but for one thing, and that one thing was monstrous. It would divide my life neatly into *before* and *after*, assuring the life I knew would never be the same again.

I cannot bear to say his name, and think of him to this day as *Asshole*. AH was nine years older than me. He lived not far from Texarkana, and my parents would visit his parents for a week once or twice every year. It was a five-hour drive, east across the top of the boot of Louisiana. The high point of the trip was always a stop at KFC. My parents, who forbade fast food at home, swooned upon opening those little red-and-white-striped boxes holding the hot, crispy chicken, warm container of mashed potatoes, buttered corn on the cob, and fluffy biscuit. I tried to appreciate the feast along with the rest of my family, but dreaded what might be coming once we reached our destination. I dabbed at the mashed potatoes with the end of my spoon, licked the butter off the corn on the cob, but couldn't bring myself to bite into it. I was too busy trying to hold back tears. I couldn't eat, hadn't slept the night before, and was terrified about what I knew was to come.

It began when AH was fifteen and I was six. It might not happen on the first day of our visit, nor the second. He would watch and wait, and when I went to the bathroom, or back into one of the bedrooms to change into my swimsuit, he would follow me and close the door behind us. I was small for

9

my age; he was practically a grown man. He was in ROTC at school and liked people to think he was smart.

He would make me sit on his lap, groping and fondling me, touching me where I did not want to be touched, forcing me to touch him. All the rest of it is too horrible to put into words, even now, all these years later.

After AH finished, he would threaten me. "If you tell your parents, they're going to hate you. They're going to stop loving you and think you're cheap trash." I believed him. I didn't have anyone to talk to or anyone to help me stop it.

One afternoon, when I was perhaps ten or eleven and he was already out of high school, he cornered me in the bathroom and pushed me into the shower, one of those stall types, slightly bigger than an old-fashioned phone booth. He undid his pants and then unzipped mine. I felt the cold tile against my back through my OshKosh B'Gosh outfit, closed my eyes, willing myself to be in another place, when suddenly I heard the bathroom door open. There stood my father.

My father was a gentle man who rarely raised his voice. Still, he was six feet tall, and he was my father. I expected him to march in, pull AH out of that shower by his collar, drag him out into the living room, and beat the living shit out of him. Instead, he stood there with his hand on the knob, looking stunned, and to my horror . . . disgusted. It was just a moment, but it dragged on for an eternity. I'll never forget it. And then he turned and left me alone in the room with AH.

I'd always been Daddy's girl. The pain of being abused was nothing compared to seeing the look in my father's eyes that day. It would haunt me for years.

I knew instantly and intuitively that even though my father had broken my heart by failing to protect me, it was over; AH had been found out. His dad was a tough and sometimes mean man, and when my dad told his dad what he'd seen, AH would get the beating of his life.

I blasted out of that shower, out of that bathroom, and ran down the hall to the back bedroom. My little suitcase was lying on the floor, and my first thought was that I should put on my swimsuit and run down the street to the home of a friend I'd made in the neighborhood, Scott. His family had a swimming pool. It was ruinously hot in the summer in east Texas, and I hadn't stopped to put on my shoes. My feet burned on the pavement. I could hear the cries and splashing of kids in the pool before I let myself in through the back gate. After a while AH had the audacity to show up and join the swim party, acting as if nothing had happened. I didn't speak to him, I didn't look at him, I didn't talk to him.

Eventually the sun slid behind the trees and all the kids were called in to dinner. Scott let me borrow a towel. I wrapped it around myself and scampered back to AH's house. My mom waited for me on the front porch. She had probably been standing there for a good hour. As I ran up, she knelt down and opened her arms, which pitched me into immediate and full-blown hysteria. I sobbed until I thought I would throw up. My father obviously had told my mother what he'd witnessed and asked her to deal with it, and as a nurse practitioner specializing in psychiatric disorders she was not unfamiliar with this kind of thing. She was calm and nurturing. She rubbed my back and kept asking what happened. To save myself, to protect myself and my sanity, I said, "It only happened once, Mommy. This was the only time."

Which was a lie. It had happened many times.

The truth would come out, but not for thirty-five years, six months before my dad passed away. As betrayed as I felt that day, I could never be truly angry at him. He was and would always be my hero. Decades later I would find out what a part of me had always suspected, that he simply couldn't handle what he had seen. He wasn't disgusted by me, as I had always thought, but rather shocked, confused, and embarrassed. Perhaps AH and I were playing doctor or experimenting. It was the seventies. Who knew what kids were up to then? Parents weren't involved in their kids' lives the way we are now. They lacked information. They lacked the tools of communication. But finally I would hear the words that gave me the strength to begin to heal: "Cathy, I wish I had protected you. I'm so sorry, baby."

But that day, I felt utterly alone. After my mom tried to soothe it away, I walked through the screen door, through the living room, in my bathing suit, clutching the towel around me, the soles of my feet burned. As I passed, the adults just said, "Hey," as if it were any lazy summer afternoon.

When I examine what drives me, this childhood trauma floats to the surface. I've learned that while I'm blessed with people in my life whom I love and who love me, I walk through this world alone, that I'm the only one responsible for taking care of myself. On that day so long ago, this thought began to take form: my parents can't protect me, my brothers can't protect me, and my friends can't, either. I put on my own armor.

I refuse to give AH any credit for the good things in my life. But one of the reasons I am able to be fearless, to work hard and stay determined over weeks, months, and years, is my refusal to be done in by shame and guilt. After it was behind me, in the weeks and months that followed the day my dad stumbled into that room and stopped it, an attitude rose up in me: "Just watch what I'm going to do now."

— two —

In grade school I developed an affection for tea parties. My mom patiently brewed decaf tea and helped me assemble the mixture for the cookies. I'd make them myself, pressing the thick, chilly dough through a cookie press that I'd discovered in one of the kitchen drawers. The press had interchangeable disks—shamrocks, stars, and hearts—and I'd make cookies in all the shapes. Then I'd put on my dress and gloves and set the table with my plastic tea service and small yellow cookies and see who I could con into sitting in one of my little-kid chairs.

I graduated from tea parties to an Easy-Bake Oven and decided I needed to expand my customer base beyond my family. I resolved to hold bake sales on the weekend, and was quite the marketer. I'd ride my bike around the neighborhood announcing my sale, then start production, one vanilla cake with chocolate frosting after the next. I set my price at five cents a cake. My sole customer was a boy from the neighborhood, Mark, who showed up with a pocketful of nickels. He put a nickel on my table and I slid him a piece of cake on a paper plate. He ate the cake, and then put down another nickel, and I slid him another. He may have been my only customer, but he was a very satisfied one.

I would one day discover the principles of opening your

own restaurant were pretty much the same: take care to create an excellent, consistent menu and treat your customers well.

⟶

My parents loved and cooked fusion food long before anyone had ever heard of it: Greek and southern.

My dad was born two months after his family arrived in Greenville, Mississippi, from Skopelos, Greece. A small, verdant island in the northern Aegean, it was founded, according to Greek mythology, by Staphylus, one of the sons of Dionysus, god of wine and the grape harvest. From my dad's side of the family came recipes for my favorite dish—now and forever—*kota kapama*, chicken cooked slowly in onions, garlic, cinnamon, and tomato paste. Served with buttery long macaroni, or over rice or orzo, this dish is the ultimate comfort food, at once savory and sophisticated and homey. My dad's family also brought *horiatiki*, tomato, cucumber, and feta salad, with a tangy vinaigrette made with red wine vinegar and fresh olive oil; a hearty *spanakopita*, a flaky savory pastry made with loads of fresh spinach, dill, and fresh parsley; *moussaka*, baked eggplant with meat and béchamel sauce made with *kefalotyri*, a salty goat cheese beloved in Greece; and *galaktoboureko*, a dessert made with delicate layers of phyllo dough and creamy vanilla custard, and topped with a hot lemon sauce—it's like crème brûlée baked in its own pastry crust.

Glistening dark-purple kalamatas were the preferred olive, feta the preferred cheese. You couldn't buy these ingredients in Mississippi in the late 1960s. You couldn't buy Greek olive oil. My dad had them shipped from Chicago.

My mom was an air force brat who grew up on bases across the country, in Tokyo, and in Honolulu. She cooked sweet-

and-sour pork, lasagna, enchiladas, and beef stroganoff. She loved to steam artichokes, and following a classic southern impulse, added homemade mustard and bourbon to her pork roasts. Out of her kitchen on Swan Lake Drive came grits and feta, spring onion, fennel and potato soup, and southern-style greens finished with Greek olive oil.

To get our pure, undiluted southern fix we visited Aunt Inez and Uncle George, my dad's half brother. They lived in Greenville, a hundred miles due northwest from Jackson. Uncle George was a furniture salesman, and as far as I could tell, Aunt Inez spent her days raising her kids, smoking, and cooking—in that order. I loved visiting them because Greenville felt like the deep, mysterious South in a way Jackson— the state's largest city and its capital, with its nationally ranked colleges and universities, museums, recording studios, and fine-dining restaurants—never quite did. Greenville is in the Mississippi Delta, what some people call "the most southern place on earth." Aunt Inez would create a real southern spread: creamed corn, mounds of fried chicken, and turnip greens. Even though her cooking was as Deep South as you could get, she had absorbed a few Greek influences from being married to George. Her biscuits and feta was top-notch.

We made the hundred-plus-mile drive several times a year, up Highway 49, through Yazoo City and Indianola, or up Highway 61 and the heart of the Delta. My dad drove the blue, wood-paneled station wagon, my mother in the passenger seat, me in the backseat in the middle between Mike and Chris. We passed miles of cotton fields and the cottonseed oil processing plants that smelled like freshly baked bread. "Let's stop at the bakery!" I'd say when I was small, certain that what I was smelling was a tray of biscuits fresh from the oven. My dad tried to explain that it was only the odor of cottonseed oil, but I refused to believe him. "Let's stop for some bread!" I'd say, stubborn like I was.

In Greenville, Aunt Inez would greet us with a plate of hot tamales. She bought them around the corner from an African American man who'd sold them from a stand for fifty years. He steamed them right there, wrapped them in newspaper, and tied the package with twine. I remember the warmth of the tamale in my hand, the softness of the *masa* (corn dough), the spicy pork or beef inside.

After Dad popped a few tamales into his mouth, he and Uncle George would grab their cane fishing poles and vanish, leaving my mom and Aunt Inez to deal with my brothers and me and our three cousins: Sharon, Brenda, and Pete. Our moms tossed us out of the house, and we would entertain ourselves running around until we fell down. Then we would climb one of the ancient magnolia trees whose thick branches reached over the street behind their house and throw seed pods, big as hand grenades, at passing cars. Once we found an empty red purse in the back of Brenda's closet and set about tricking passing motorists. We tied the purse to a fishing reel and slung it out into the middle of the road, the clear fishing line invisible. You can bet every car that came along stopped to check it out. We hid in the underbrush, watching as the driver climbed out of his car, and just as he reached down to pick up the purse, whoever's turn it was to hold the rod would reel in the purse. We'd scoop up the purse and then run away, cackling like maniacs.

⁓

In the home kitchens of my youth everyone cooked from scratch. No one used cake mixes, Hamburger Helper, or even Kraft Macaroni & Cheese. My mom, busy as she was with her full-time nursing job, made her own pizza dough and piecrusts. Her mother, Grandmom Alma, turned out beautiful cheesecakes and pies until she was well into her nineties. When we would visit Alma in Texas, she spent the day before our departure making deviled ham and date bars dusted with powdered sugar for our trip home. Neither my mom nor my grandmom believed in fast food, which was the definition of good money after bad. They were ahead of their time, both absolutely confident that they could easily whip up something better tasting, more nourishing, and less expensive.

Historically, in Jackson, the Greeks were the restaurant people. Along with the Italians they brought fine dining to the area. By the end of the sixties, all but two of the fine-dining establishments in Jackson were owned by Greeks. The Elite was owned by the Zoboukas, and the Dennery clan owned and ran Dennery's. The Mayflower was opened in 1935 by the Kountouris and Gouras families, and is still owned by a Kountouris. It's the oldest continuously operating restaurant in Jackson, famous for its spicy, garlicky Comeback Sauce that keeps you coming back for more.

When the Karagiozoses came through Ellis Island in the 1930s, the name was shortened to Cora. Grandpa Pete Cora settled in Greenville in 1935 and opened a little place called The Coney Island Cafe, a name he chose because he thought it sounded American.

There was another important Pete in my family, Peter J. Costas, otherwise known as Godfather Pete, whom everyone called Taki, and who owned a white-tablecloth restaurant called the Continental. Godfather Pete was one of my father's great friends. Before the Continental, he'd owned the popular Shamrock Drive-Inn, where he introduced the concept of the take-out slice of pizza to Jackson and my parents to each other. My dad managed the place and had a reputation for flirting with the nursing students who frequented it. Before my mom, he dated a girl in the class behind her—William Faulkner's niece, Avis.

The Continental was magical, with its big red leather booths, the clinking of the silverware and china, the *whoosh* of people racing around with purpose, the smell of fish seared in a pan, steak tossed on the grill, the garlicky bread smell of pizza baking. People could smoke in restaurants back then, and a glamorous cloud of cigarette smoke hung over the dining room. The menu was what was then called continental. Spaghetti and meatballs, shrimp scampi, crab Louie, and London broil.

My parents, a schoolteacher and a nurse, didn't make much money, so they were frugal. The Continental was for special occasions only, the most common one being their wedding anniversary. They always brought my brothers and me along, reasoning that if they were going to have to fork out money for a babysitter anyway, they may as well pay for us to enjoy a good meal.

My dad liked to walk me back into the kitchen, where he would set me on the counter. I would swing my legs and the cooks would ask, "What do you want to eat, baby?" I was no prodigy of haute cuisine. I wanted fried chicken or a hamburger, but my dad would coax me into expanding my palate. "You can have a hamburger anytime!" he'd say (not entirely true). "Order shrimp, order steak!"

My dad wasn't merely urging me to expand my palate. He and my mom believed that enjoying a wide variety of food was part of being a cultivated person. Even though we didn't have much money, it was important to them that my brothers and I learn to appreciate culture. They saved up for season tickets for the symphony one year, and another time we drove to New Orleans to see the King Tut exhibit. My parents were always interested in furthering our aesthetic education, as long as it was within driving distance.

⁓

As children, we have no point of comparison for our parents. All I knew was that my mom was always there for her family, no more devoted to her nurse job than any other grown-up with a job. Only much later would I learn the degree to which she was devoted to her profession. My mom was a model of hard work. I sensed her intelligence, stamina, and great reserve of energy. I knew that she never missed a day of work, and didn't believe in burnout. She believed in *rest*, but she also found nursing to be invigorating. One of the post–master's certificates she eventually earned qualified her to teach the same courses she'd just aced to new nursing students. Once someone asked her why she took on this job and she said, "We needed someone to teach that curriculum, I was interested, so I just put my head down and did it." Her final degree count is a bachelor's and two master's degrees from the University of Mississippi School of Nursing, a master's from Mississippi University for Women, and eventually, a doctorate from the University of Alabama at Birmingham.

If my mom showed me what it was like to live with passion for your chosen profession, my dad gave me a taste of being a citizen of the world. I knew we were "half Greek" because of Dad, and that knowledge made him more glamorous than the other dads in the neighborhood. Often, perhaps once a month, during some strange time of the day—very late at night or early in the morning—I would hear him talking on the phone to his family in Greece. He would be speaking loudly, in another language, and nothing struck me as more exotic.

He owned a huge atlas and we'd sit down at the kitchen table and he showed me where the Karagiozoses lived, on a little island called Skopelos. I loved that big, full-colored atlas. I can still see the irregular outline of Europe. France was spring green. Greece, just east of pale yellow Italy, was dusky purple.

If there was one thing I loved more than food, it was stories that would carry me to somewhere far away from Swan Lake Drive. Among my peers I felt alone in my perception that loving literature was a way of loving the larger world. I had big plans, and these plans made me something of an outcast. I had a secret list of goals and dreams. I would live in New York, travel to Paris.

My dad indulged my curiosity, even when it cost him. I liked to make things with junk I came across in the storage room. Once I made a sculpture of a woman out of plaster with one of my dad's drill bits. Any other child would have received a good whuppin'. That was a thirty-dollar drill bit. He was dismayed at my ingenuity but also impressed, and I think maybe he felt the cost had been worth it.

did it up to her liking, complete with floral wallpaper and a dust ruffle on the bed. She spent her days producing a nonstop stream of classic egg salads and chicken salads, stupendous cheesecakes, and for our birthdays, her silky Italian cream cake with not-too-sweet cream cheese frosting. She did not belong to the church of Chores Build Character, and merrily washed and folded our clothes and deposited them in our drawers and in all other ways spoiled us.

As her only granddaughter I was her favorite. There is no sense pretending otherwise. I reveled in her presence. I appointed myself her assistant cheesecake maker. I assembled the ingredients, dusted the springform pan with sugar, and grated the lemon zest.

I loved her beyond measure, and one of my cherished early memories is of her feeding me. I'm sitting on the floor in front of a TV. Bright colors, a warm ocean breeze on my naked arms. Suddenly, a white bowl descends from above my head like a spaceship and lands in my lap. The feel of the plastic is smooth on my knees. I scoop up one of the cold, pale orange squares in the bowl and press it into my mouth with the flat of my hand. The juice squirts out over my bottom lip and down my chin. The taste is sweet, but light and slippery. Not cookie sweet, not rough and dry. Fresh. Grandmom has given me my first taste of cantaloupe, freshly cut and cubed. I am no older than three.

My close relationship with Alma complicated things with my brothers. Chris and I were thirteen months apart, and our personalities clashed. My closeness with Alma strained our relationship further, despite the truce we'd managed to achieve. We were just so different. He was a calm and collected boy

~ three ~

The same year I started high school my mom went back to school. She once said that whenever she reached a crossroads in life, she would add either a baby to the family or another degree. In this case, the crossroads was having three children in high school and needing more income. When she'd gone back to school before, I'd been in grammar school, and she'd been able to attend the local Jackson medical center affiliated with the University of Mississippi, but they didn't offer a nursing doctorate. The nearest place she could matriculate was at the University of Alabama in Birmingham, a good three-and-a-half-hour drive one way, so she couldn't commute. Instead, she planned to move to Birmingham, where she would live in the dorm just like any other student.

I was anxious about who was going to take care of us. In the morning I would wake up with a nervous stomach and plunge into my day as quickly as possible so as not to dwell on it, a habit I've carried into adulthood. It was one thing for a mother not to be home if she had a job, but to not be home because she decided to become a college student again? Whose mother did such a thing?

I had no idea then that all of her additional degrees were directly tied to the family income. Money was always tight and somehow just kept getting tighter. My brothers and I received one present at Christmas, one on our birthday, and a new outfit for Easter. Those gifts were the canaries in the coal mine of our family economy; the more lavish the present, the better my parents were doing.

We spent months making our Christmas lists, always from the big J. C. Penney catalog that arrived in the late spring. We knew that we would get one "big" present, which was usually our second or third choice, so we agonized over our decision, trying to figure out where on the list to put the thing we wanted most. Some years, right after Thanksgiving, my parents sat us down and said, "Kids, this isn't going to be a big Christmas." We knew they meant it. My parents always meant what they said. They saw no reason to spare us the truth, as hard as it may have been for them.

In our stockings, we always got some candy and an orange. Every year I hoped the orange was a ball, but it was always an orange. What we lacked in presents we made up for in tradition. Regardless of our finances, my parents always went the extra mile to make the holiday special. We decorated our tree while drinking hot cocoa and listening to Christmas music. We baked cookies and went caroling, and I always wound up feeling as if I had had plenty of Christmas.

To supplement our income, our dad, in addition to teaching full time, worked the high school football games, weekends at J. C. Penney, and delivered bouquets for a local florist. He especially loved the delivery job, because unlike his tenth-grade world history students, everyone was always glad to see him when he showed up with a floral arrangement. Sometimes he would even earn himself a kiss on the cheek from some extra-happy recipient.

I was equal parts scared and irritated about Mom going back to school. My parents were partners, but there was no

doubt in anyone's mind, including Dad's, that Mom kept the locomotive that was Cora family life rolling forward. Without Mom, who would flip on my bedroom light at 6:00 a.m.? Who would make our dubious jelly and mayonnaise sandwiches? Who would buy the correct laundry soap that made our clothes smell clean and familiar? Who would come out onto the porch on Saturday evenings, just as it was getting dark, and blow a whistle to summon us home?

Then one day my mom and dad sat us down on the couch and shared the solution: Grandmom Alma was going to come to live with us and run the house and keep my brothers and me out of trouble.

Both Alma and her husband, my granddad Clyde, had served in the army, and met when they were stationed at the Fitzsimons Army Hospital in Aurora, Colorado. He was a medical doctor and a first lieutenant. She was a nurse and a captain, and outranked him, a fact that tickled my mom and also inspired her.

Alma was tough, but from the moment she laid eyes on me I had her under my spell. Our mom was a firm believer in the character-building value of chores, a set bedtime, and strict schedule. By the time we hit junior high we were doing our own laundry. We all knew how to properly set the table, load and unload the dishwasher, and mow the lawn. Before we were allowed to get our driver's licenses, we had to prove to her satisfaction that we were confident changing a flat tire. She created a trio of duties, categorized by location: kitchen helper, house helper, yard helper. It wasn't gender specific and every Sunday night we rotated to the next assignment.

But when Grandmom Alma moved in during my freshman year of high school, she dispensed with all that. She delighted in taking care of us. She moved into the guest bedroom

of few words. Even though he was the younger one, he was like the old dog and I was like the puppy, always bouncing around with new enthusiasm. I'd always felt closer to Mike, and we developed a sort of coalition. Mom claimed it was because when she was in the hospital giving birth to Chris, Mike helped take care of me. The adults were consumed with the arrival of the new baby, who was three and a half weeks late (it wasn't the fashion to induce in those days), but Mike saw to it that I got my bottle and changed my diapers, and would sit on the couch and hold me on his lap. He was only in kindergarten.

Mike was a good-looking kid, gangly, with a wide smile and large brown eyes. He struggled with attention deficit disorder, for which there wasn't any real treatment in Mississippi at the time, and had been held back in fifth grade. As he got older he turned into a charmer, a rogue with a special gift for getting himself into trouble. He was a good ol' boy from the beginning, a type of male specific to Mississippi, and furthermore, as he grew up, *knew* he was that type and adopted a kind of Billy Bob Thornton *Sling Blade* persona he trotted out when he wanted to crack people up and endear himself to them.

His great love was fishing, and to get to the bream and bass, the great game fish for which our freshwater lakes are famous, he needed a boat. He could never afford to buy one, but after he got his driver's license he hatched a scheme whereby he would find someone in the classifieds who was selling a boat, call them up, and say he was interested in buying it, but would, of course, need to test-drive it first. He'd leave his license with the owner as collateral, hook the boat up to the back of his truck, then go on a fishing trip. After a few days out on the lake, he'd return the boat, saying it wasn't for him.

The owners would be justifiably enraged, which he acknowledged without exhibiting a trace of guilt. He'd just start talking fishing, and before too long they'd offer him a beer and start comparing stories, and soon they'd forget all about it. He was shameless. Once my mom was driving me home from some after-school activity and we passed him going in the opposite direction with a golf cart hitched to the back of his truck. Mom stopped, rolled down the window, and asked what he was doing. "Just checking it out! I might want one of these."

He was a genial con man, even at a young age. Mike barely graduated high school, fell in with a bad crowd, got a little too heavily into pot, and started writing bad checks. After he got caught, no amount of charm could keep him from being sent to the penal farm, the Mississippi version of juvie.

I spent several Sundays in the car with my mom, driving up to visit him. We'd go after church, and I'd bring him some pecans I'd picked off the tree beside the parking lot. I've always been emotional, and I would cry as we went through security and as we sat in the waiting room, which was as big as the school cafeteria. My mom, normally chatty, was silent. It was grim, but Mike was always happy to see us, embarrassed by his predicament only a little.

My parents spent a lot of time and energy steeped in concern about him and his struggles, leaving Chris and me to fend for ourselves a bit. Chris stayed as far away from the Mike situation as possible, hiding beneath the covers on Sunday mornings, leaving the house to hang with his friends. I dealt with the relative lack of attention by daydreaming about what I would do when I was on my own, far from Jackson, in some exotic place doing something exciting, as yet unknown.

My grammar school days playing softball had awakened in me twin urges for competition and for being part of a team. I tried out for and made the Wingfield Follies, our school musical revue, every fall, which required long hours after school spent painting sets, making costumes, learning our lines and routines. I served on the student council, was secretary/treasurer of the Junior Classical League (a club for students taking Latin), and a member of MYGA, Mississippi Youth and Government, and continued to play softball every spring.

It's unfashionable to look back fondly on high school, but I enjoyed myself. Wingfield had a precision drill team called the Genteels that every girl in the school who was even remotely coordinated tried out for. The Genteels were mostly juniors and seniors, but every year a few sophomores were chosen, and I was one of three who was tapped that year. It was very prestigious. I loved working out the complicated routines, and also the outfits: sparkly blue hot pants worn with a long, puffy-sleeved white blouse and a sparkly gold vest. The ensemble was completed with gloves and knee-high white leather boots with two-inch heels. I had a good haircut with feathered bangs. My mom has kept the documentation of these days, of my bad perms, amateur makeup application, and fifteen extra pounds in a photo album. She loves these pictures as only a mother can. I look back and marvel with amazement that I look and feel better at forty-seven than I did at eighteen.

The common wisdom holds that a chef's life begins in a kitchen, and while there was no doubt my family loved food—whenever my mom was home on the weekend we cooked nonstop, dishes like *kota kapama* with noodles and boiled greens drizzled with olive oil and garlic, and my dad would often fire up the smoker and make some of his locally famous beef brisket—a lot of these high school extracurriculars, as silly as they may seem in retrospect, instilled in me a love of working hard with a team all focused on a single outcome. Without knowing it, I was developing the skills I would one day need to work in a professional kitchen.

While in high school I also got myself a boyfriend, Johnny.

He was tall and thin, brown haired with wide-set brown eyes, and ears a little too large for his head. Johnny was serious for his age. He had a wretched home life; his alcoholic father was in and out of the picture, and even in tenth grade, Johnny had an after-school job as a stock boy at a local department store to help support his family. We were an item for the duration of high school. One year we shook things up at the junior prom by wearing matching formal wear. Black trousers, white notched tailcoat, red bow tie. He bought me a red carnation corsage for my lapel. This was seriously daring for Jackson, Mississippi, in the early 1980s, and damn if I didn't look better in my tux than in a gold taffeta gown.

When Johnny and I met I was already sure I preferred girls, but equally certain that it hardly mattered, because like every good southern girl, I would grow up, find the best man I could, marry him, and have a passel of kids. I didn't even fantasize about being truly, deeply in love with a girlfriend because I knew I could never have it. It would be like a straight chick hoping to marry a rock star or the Prince of Wales. Even though my family was nice enough to Dalton and Millard, the gay couple across the street, I knew that people like me had to keep what was in their hearts secret.

I've no doubt that part of my urge to overload my schedule was tied up in coping with my sexuality, in channeling all that hormonal confusion. I also stayed busy because otherwise I would fall into a funk. Day after day, all over my high school, I would see girls with their boyfriends, holding hands, stealing a kiss between classes. It was no secret how attracted they were to each other, how happy they were. I had not one complaint with Johnny, but I could never cajole myself into feeling anything other than fondness. Even when we were making out I would be thinking about my next day's to-do list.

To make some spending money I got a job working part-time as counter help at the Peanut Shack, a kiosk in the Metrocenter Mall in south Jackson that sold candy, caramel popcorn balls, and chocolate chip cookies the size of your head. At home, I augmented Alma's perfect cheesecakes with junk food from my job.

My mom may have been gone during the week and consumed with her studies, but she could take one look at me and know something was wrong, even though she couldn't imagine what it might be. On her weekends home she'd watch me, taking note of my despondent expressions, my inclination to lock myself in my room for long stretches of time. She was ahead of her time, sang the praises of endorphins, and suggested my mood might perk right up with a jog around the block. When that didn't work she suggested Prozac.

I didn't like her suggestion. I was outraged in the way that judgy teenagers tend to be. *Prozac?* Was I truly that messed up? Was she suggesting I get a lobotomy, too? I hadn't reached a point where I could formulate a rebuttal, even in my own mind. I was nowhere close to being able to say to myself or anyone else that if I could just be free to pursue girls I wouldn't be forced to tamp down my true feelings with beer and chocolate.

Then, when I was seventeen, Jordan happened.

~ four ~

The summer between my junior and senior year I worked as a lifeguard at the YMCA pool. The Bryan Adams song "Summer of '69" was big on Jackson radio around that time, and it was the perfect anthem. I remember that summer was hot, but not so humid and buggy. In the mornings I'd sit high up in my lifeguard chair, feel the sun on my legs, holler at the occasional kid to quit messing around, inhale the warm smell of newly mown lawns.

I bought a used car with my savings from the Peanut Shack, a red Fiat X1/9. My normally easygoing dad had come out firmly against it. "Don't do it. Don't buy it. That car will spend its life in the shop." I revered my dad's levelheadedness and patience. I knew he never offered his opinion if he wasn't pretty sure he was right. But I ignored him regarding the car. I was a lifeguard, and it was a hot little red convertible. There was no convincing me.

Jordan lived not far from the pool, and she came over most mornings for a swim. She was stunning, with wavy blond hair, a turned-up nose, and pageant queen smile. Perched in my lifeguard chair, I'd watch her gleaming body glide through the water from behind my Ray-Bans. After she did a few laps she would lie out on the pool deck and we would talk aimlessly about school. She was a cheerleader and I was on the drill team, so we had that in common. Every morning as she walked through the gate, my palms got sweaty. Every afternoon when I got off work, I fantasized about her all the way home, my tape deck blasting the Tears for Fears hit "Shout." My car smelled like sweat and coconut oil, and I sang at the top of my lungs, "Shout, shout, let it all out . . ."

That year break dancing had arrived in Jackson. The year before, *Flashdance* had been in the local theaters, and Michael Jackson moonwalking was all the rage. One day I was telling Jordan about a break-dancing group I'd joined, and she asked if I could come over to her house after I got off work and show her some moves.

I can't remember where her parents were, but they must have been at work. She put in a cassette tape from the movie *Breakin'*, and I taught her what I knew and then, like in the movies, a slow song came on, and there was that awkward moment when you either pretended you were finished dancing or else you went for it and draped yourself all over the other person. It was Jordan's idea. I wouldn't have dared. We danced for a while. Even though a box air-conditioner whirred in one of the windows, we were still sweaty and overheated from dancing.

I don't remember who went after whom, but suddenly, just like that, we started kissing. In a minute, we were a tangle of arms, hair, mouth, and tongue. We started grinding to the music. Her taste was Crest toothpaste, her smell Coppertone. Her hair was heavy in my hands.

I felt like a human sparkler, every inch of me bright and crackling. My ears rang, the room spun. I thought kissing Jordan just might kill me. *This* was what it was supposed to be like. This was what all the love songs were about.

The rest of the summer we were inseparable. To the world

it looked as if we'd just struck up one of those intense friendships teenage girls are famous for. No one questioned that I wanted to be with her every spare moment. I couldn't eat, couldn't sleep. Every song on the radio described our desperate love.

Johnny hadn't been around much anyhow. He'd graduated from Wingfield the year before and started working for Lowe's Home Improvement. I broke up with him, offering the usual lame it's-me-not-you, I-think-we-should-see-other-people nonsense, but it was to be with Jordan.

Jordan and I cruised up and down McDowell Boulevard in my Fiat with the top down, radio blaring, hair snarling in the wind. We'd stop at Pizza Hut to fix ourselves in the mirror, hang out in the air-conditioning, and nurse Diet Dr Peppers. We'd go on what I thought of as proper dates, mostly to the movies, but of course there was no hand holding in public, even in the dark.

My brother Mike, who'd served his time at the penal farm, was living in a trailer on the outskirts of town. I told him Jordan and I were double dating and needed a place to make out with our guys. A lie, of course.

When we drove up to the empty trailer I was sweating every place a person can sweat. It was easy to blame the nonstop sauna that is a Mississippi summer, but the truth was that I was nervous. Jordan chattered away, hiding her nerves with bright banter. I'd never made love to a woman and neither had she. Now, the thing we had been waiting for seemed all but impossible to accomplish. As I imagined going down on her, I kept thinking about a conversation between Mike and his friends, about how bad their hands smelled after they'd finger-fucked their girlfriends. I could not get that thought out of my mind. What if this thing I'd been waiting for seemingly forever was funky and gross? What if, when I got down there, I actually gagged?

My hands shook a little as I threaded Mike's key into the lock. He had thoughtfully left some windows open, but there was no air-conditioning and the metal siding creaked in the heat. The trailer was like a very large tin can roasting in the sun. I looked at Jordan and she took a deep breath and reached over for my hand. It was clear that this would be our only shot in the foreseeable future. A little heat was nothing.

We fumbled around, me trying to unhook her bra, her grabbing my ass. Somehow we got our clothes off. Jordan's taste was the opposite of funky and gross. She was a little salty and musky. It reminded me of oysters. I'd tried my first one when I was ten years old, at Felix's Restaurant and Oyster Bar in New Orleans. I'd resisted at first, then was surprised with joy at its slick, briny goodness.

I just about gave myself heatstroke trying to satisfy Jordan, but eventually we both came. Finally I knew what it was to make love.

Jordan and I lasted all summer, and two months into the school year. In hindsight our association had summer romance written all over it, but I was as stubborn then as I am now, and was determined to make it last as long as I could. I leveraged my power as her chauffeur, picking her up in the mornings and delivering her to her front door at the end of the day. If cheerleading practice went longer than drill team practice, I waited.

Then one day I heard some gossip I pretended to ignore: Jordan had a crush on a guy whose name I can't recall, who everyone agreed was superhot. To make matters more awkward, my brother Chris, who was also a cheerleader, told me one night after we did the dishes that he was thinking about asking Jordan out.

"She's not really your type," I said, stooping to put the Tupperware in a low cupboard, the better to hide my expression. "She doesn't treat guys very well. I don't think she'd be good for you." I was a little proud of myself for telling him the truth without revealing anything.

The rumors about Jordan and the hot guy persisted, and one afternoon after school I confronted her. It was deep into fall. I remember the hazy bronze sky, the smoke smell from people burning their leaves.

"We're just friends," she said.

A lie, of course. In my heart I knew immediately.

I went home, threw myself onto my bed, and sobbed. I cried daily for what seemed like weeks on end. Chris was busy with his own life, and just assumed, I think, that I was one more inexplicable girl. Grandmom Alma thought a boy might be to blame. My dad was perplexed, but he was Greek, and understood in his DNA that even though he was soft-spoken, passionate outbursts were nothing to get too excited over. My friends at school were mystified, concerned, and finally just sort of thought I'd lost my mind.

In the South, people say "bless her heart" for a number of reasons, none of which has anything to do with praying that God bestows his grace upon your cardiovascular system. Bless her heart is the preamble when you're about to say something disapproving about someone, and also when someone's behavior is so peculiar that some form of undiagnosed mental illness is the only explanation. I have no doubt that a lot of bless your hearts were said behind my back the autumn of my senior year.

I threw myself back into my extracurriculars, and also tried out for Gayfer Girls. Gayfers was a department store across the South (it eventually was bought out by Dillard's), and

Gayfer Girls were the teen advisory board whose job it was to give advice to customers on the latest fashions, produce fashion shows, and serve as Gayfer ambassadors in various charity events around Mississippi. Because it is impossible to be a member of something in the Deep South without there being a special outfit involved, Gayfer Girls were issued a red blazer and hat, and a red, orange, gray, and cream–patterned scarf. I didn't appreciate the rich aptness of the name *Gay*fer Girl at the time, which was just as well.

Like everyone else, Johnny had assumed Jordan was just my new best friend. What I'd always liked about him I liked even more now: he could tell something was different about me, but he didn't pressure me to explain myself. I was grateful to him, but also miserable.

He was now a manager at Lowe's, traveling around the South training staff how to be managers. After Jordan broke up with me, Johnny and I got back together. He suggested we meet at El Chico, a Mexican chain restaurant popular in the South that we both liked. When I arrived he was holding a sign and had a bouquet of balloons, as if I'd come home from a long trip abroad. Over dessert he gave me a promise ring, which I accepted without hesitation.

My relationship with Jordan had been so painful. She was my first love. I saw how trying to love a woman would be too hard for me, too fraught. With men I could play the role, well aware that I wasn't being touched at my deepest level. With Johnny I could be the girlfriend and look happy. He was a sweet guy who would take care of me. I thought, *Well, this is it.* I was prepared to go quietly into that good night and accept my fate. I was ready to marry him, this sweet, honest guy who didn't deserve any of this.

~ five ~

No matter how terrible I felt—and I assure you, these were difficult times—when I walked into the kitchen and started opening the cupboards, everything inside me settled. I learned that if I put my head down and paid attention only to the food, peace would follow. When I had a free evening I liked to cook for my godparents, Taki and Maria. Taki had long since sold the Continental, but he knew his recipe for herb, lemon, and garlic chicken by heart, and delighted in tossing on an apron and giving me a few pointers.

Taki had learned his trade in Lyon, France, during World War II. Lyon, not Paris, was the true birthplace of French cuisine. So groundbreaking was Lyon, that in the sixteenth century the food of Lyonnais chefs was thought to rival that of their Florentine counterparts, and in the nineteenth century the female chefs of Lyon started opening their own restaurants (unheard of). Madame Brazier, a Lyon native, was the first woman to win three Michelin stars twice, and went on to train Lyon's most famous chef, and one of the most revered chefs on earth, Paul Bocuse.

Taki made his way across Europe from his native Greece and put himself through university working in restaurants, starting out washing dishes, then moving up to prep work. Lyon's white-tablecloth restaurants were not exempt from the postwar food shortages. Often he would come to work at dawn, only to find they had run out of salt or flour, and the chef would send him out to scrounge some up, using his own money. Even though he spent long hours in the kitchen, he often went hungry. Some days his meals consisted of a piece of bread and a small wedge of cheese.

Taki taught me how to cure salmon and how to make the best lyonnaise dressing, with chopped shallots, Dijon mustard, red wine vinegar, and olive oil. Together we made beautifully roasted chicken, golden brown and succulent, the way they did in the bistros in Paris I had read about. He patiently demonstrated how to season, sauté, and flambé. Sometimes my dad would get into the act and bust out his sensational shrimp pilaf or stuffed bell peppers. Or we'd all work elbow-to-elbow, happily chopping and slicing to prepare a Greek country salad and stuffed grape leaves.

As I was cooking with Taki and my dad, my mom was away at the University of Alabama. She was a teaching assistant and also a research fellow, which meant she was expected to devote herself to her studies and forgo a regular paycheck while she was earning her degree. We couldn't afford such a luxury, so every other weekend when she drove back home from Birmingham, she picked up a few twelve-hour shifts at the rehab hospital. This remained her schedule for my entire high school career, and after the first bloom of having my dad and grandmom to myself, I found myself resenting her absence, which bled into resenting her in general for the sexual abuse I'd suffered at the hands of AH and how its aftermath was handled.

After the truth came to light on that humid summer afternoon not far from Texarkana, when I was perhaps ten or eleven, it was shoved into darkness again. Many of us who have been abused know this: even after the abuse ends, you remain stuck in that time, that place, with all that shame. Your loved ones, relieved that the abuse has been exposed, hope and assume that your psychic wound will heal, like any other injury. The passage of time, combined with my mom's habit of always focusing on the positive and her determination to keep the peace at all costs, turned my abuse, which everyone had known about, talked about, and presumably accepted, back into a dark secret. My mom was a psychiatric nurse pursuing her PhD, and she never asked me whether I was still troubled by my experience. The irony was not lost on me.

By the time my mom finished her doctoral program, everyone was fed up with her absence. What had originally seemed like a good solution to the family's financial problems had begun to annoy my dad. His mother-in-law had effectively replaced his beloved life partner—which is not to say my dad didn't love and appreciate Alma, it just wasn't what he signed up for.

If there was an issue, my dad and Alma had to figure it out, or he had to wait until my mom was free to talk on the phone. It was a good decade before cell phones and computers were commonplace, and in any case my mom was in class much of the time. He dealt with teenagers all day long, then he had to come home and deal with us. No wonder he was losing his patience.

Sometimes when my mom was home I would hear them "having a discussion" in the next room, and it would evolve quickly into a full-blown argument. I never could hear enough to understand what exactly they were fighting about, but now that I have a spouse who stays home with the children while I spend a lot of time on the road, I understand what they must have been going through: they missed each other, and they were disconnected, and they were both depleted.

My inauspicious college career began under this domestic cloud. I was the living, breathing definition of clueless, and I had an incurable case of the fuck-its. My friend Sandy was going to nearby Hinds Community College and living in the dorms and asked me to be her roommate. I didn't see why not. What else was I going to do? I had been a B student in high school. My college degree–crazed parents believed with dread and certainty that I would skip out on college, and going to Hinds was a good compromise.

Early on I discovered I had an aptitude for drinking. I started with the easy stuff—beer. Eventually I would discover Crown Royal and Diet Coke, and later still, the virtues of a good wine. But back then, a Mississippi girl looking for a buzz had three options: Miller Lite, Coors Lite, and Bud Lite. Without much effort, Sandy and I were able to find a party to get drunk at most nights of the week.

The yard helper/house helper/kitchen helper rules my mom had enforced when my brothers and I were in grade school had long since been dropped, and the other basic chores I used to do before my mom went off to get her PhD were a dim memory. I'd become used to being waited on, living in a house with miraculously dust-free surfaces, and wearing clothing that magically washed and folded itself and appeared in a neat pile in the center of my apparently self-making bed. I'd become soft, spoiled, and petulant. And a picnic to be around, I'm sure.

Without Alma on duty to provide nourishing meals, I gained weight. Cooking in our dorm room consisted of heating up soup and making Top Ramen in an electric hot pot Sandy and I had bought. One night I came home late, drunk, and hungry. Sandy was still out with her friends. I found a can of ravioli, opened it, dumped it into the hot pot, cranked that sucker up to high, then decided I was in desperate need of a shower. After the shower, I was exhausted and fell into bed.

In the morning, I awoke to the smell of burned tomato paste and the sound of Sandy swearing. The hot pot was ruined. Overnight the ravioli had been transformed from something marginally edible to a concrete slab you might employ in building a prison. The incident was a metaphor for everything that was wrong with my life, and my parents, who were busy but not completely oblivious, insisted I move home. I'm sure they were worried I'd wind up like many wayward Mississippi girls, pregnant and without direction.

By my nineteenth birthday I was out of the closet, at least in my head. My family and high school friends knew nothing about my personal life, and I didn't have any gay friends. But I'd started working at a bodybuilding gym—not a health club, but a serious, no-frills gymnasium, complete with clanking weight plates, booming music, and the tangy smell of sweat. There I met some gay people. Some gay *women*. I had found my tribe, sort of. At least I didn't have to focus on keeping my desires a secret around them. They introduced me to the lone lesbian bar in Jackson, a hole-in-the-wall within walking distance of the capitol building, and one weekend we drove to New Orleans after work and I had a torrid one-night stand with a smokin' hot girl named Holly.

The night I officially came out was nothing I'd planned. It was a typical humid Mississippi summer night. The air smelled of dying grass. Frogs hopped around on our back patio. They appeared every evening just after sunset, attracted to who knows what. I'd gotten myself gussied up, and my mom and dad thought I was going to meet a bunch of girls from school for a drink. In reality, I was going on a blind date with Holly. I've always liked girly girls, an uncommon preference back in the dyke era of the old lesbian South. Her name was Holly, and it turned out she was the cousin of a woman in Jackson known around town as the Queen of the Lesbians. She was a full-blooded southern eccentric who'd opened an oyster bar with family money.

When I met Holly in Jackson, I knew immediately it wasn't going to happen. Maybe what we'd felt before had been the sexy buzz of being in New Orleans, mingled with the cheap drinks. Back in Jackson, things between us were comically awkward. She might as well have been straight.

I came home miserable and steeped in self-pity. The house was dark, the hum of the central air-conditioning the loneliest sound on earth. My situation crashed down upon me. This was what it was going to be like for the rest of my life. Lying about where I went and with whom. Lying about whom I loved. Lying about who I was.

My parents and Grandmom Alma were at a dinner party down the street. My mom and I had been butting heads of late. Some of it was the usual stuff: I had a few too many ear piercings for her taste, and also sported a silver ear cuff that she despised. My brothers, even with Mike's behavior problems and Chris's occasional surliness, were simple southern boys she could handle. They were buttoned up and she was buttoned up and I wanted to express myself. Plus, I was holding her secretly responsible for everything in my life that was going wrong.

Still, when everything felt the most bleak I wanted my mom. I knew they would be home in a few hours, but I was bursting. This could not wait another minute. Without giving it a thought I picked up the phone and called her.

"I need to talk to you right now!" I said. Hearing the urgency in my own voice caused me to start crying.

"Right now?" she said. "It can't wait?"

"No!" I said.

"Are you okay?"

"I'm not hurt. I'm okay. But no, I'm not okay." As the words left my mouth I knew they made no sense.

I went into my bedroom and threw myself facedown on my bed, waiting to hear the sound of the front door. I didn't have to wait long.

"What's going on?" my mom said. She sat down on the edge of my bed.

"I think I'm gay!" I cried. I had no doubt that I was gay, but I impulsively added *I think* to soften the blow, both for my mom and for me. I'd never said anything remotely like this aloud, not even to Jordan.

"Well . . ." she said, buying herself a little time, putting on her psychiatric nurse bedside manner. "How do you know?"

"I went on a date with a girl tonight. And I wanted it to be so good and it was so bad! What am I going to do?"

"You're not going to worry about it at all," said my mom.

I cried until my eyes were swollen shut, so relieved to be no longer alone in my secret. I didn't have to hide whom I was attracted to; whom I liked a little; whom I loved; who, one day, would be my soul mate. After years of hiding I was out, but also worried what Dad and Grandmom would say. Both of them were more traditional than my mom, and this was the Deep South. Mississippi is one of the least progressive states when it comes to gay people. The state doesn't recognize same-sex marriages, same-sex couples are not allowed to adopt, there are no laws against discrimination against gay people, and there is no hate-crime legislation. On the night I came out to my mom, same-sex sexual activity was illegal, and would remain so until 2003. I could have been arrested and tossed in jail for having dated Jordan.

My mom rubbed my back until I stopped hiccupping, then called my dad to say she would see them at home. She sat on the edge of my bed and we talked until I fell asleep, relieved that after holding in my secret, the truth was out. Somewhere between then and the next day she broke the news to each of them, separately, and the response was weirdly identical: "It doesn't matter. She's still our girl."

Confessing to my mom had brought me some relief, but I remained depressed by my options. Most of the women I came across in Jackson who were fully out were pretty butch and not what I was attracted to at all. I started dating Deborah, who lived in Biloxi. She was a good twenty years older than me, and still closeted. She had long blond hair and a strong bone structure, handsome without being masculine, the way some women are. Her sister was the only person who knew she was gay, and once Deborah had come out to her the subject was never mentioned again, to the point where it was as if she'd never come out at all.

I'd drive down on the weekends to see her. The highway south was as dark as any wilderness at night. I felt lonely and crazy, tooling south in my little red Fiat. I'd arrive and we'd go to a bar with her straight friends, play footsie under the table, then sneak off to some crazy-ass apartment—I never knew whom it belonged to—so we could fumble around. It was all so tawdry and sad. I yearned to fall in love, to find my soul mate.

My mom became increasingly concerned about AIDS. Since she worked in the health field, she was more aware than most people I knew, but still, in 1986, little was known about the disease, especially in Mississippi. It was thought only gay men and intravenous drug users contracted it, but my mom worried. If gay men got it, couldn't gay women get it, too? We started having arguments every time I got dressed up to go out. She feared that I was sleeping with every lesbian who would have me. This was so far from the truth it drove me crazy, and I would lose my temper. I was as picky as a fairy-tale princess, and despite all the making out and groping, practically still a virgin.

She'd also read somewhere that lesbians often resorted to wearing lavender to signal they were free and wanting to hook up. The Gap and the Limited and all the stores I frequented were showing purple that year. I came home with a lavender pantsuit and my mom let out a shriek like she just heard someone had died. Her face turned the color people associate with heart attack or stroke. She was bouncing on her toes, practically levitating. "Oh my God, what on earth are you doing? When you go out in . . . in . . . *that*, every girl you come across is going to think what you're saying is 'I want sex! I want a lover!'" She babbled on about Lesbos and the Greek goddesses. I had no idea what this lady was talking about. The cool, liberal psychiatric nurse I knew as my mom had been replaced by a wild-eyed wacko.

"What are you talking about? Lavender is in style. It's in fashion. It's a *trend*."

We stood in the kitchen and hollered at each other for a while. If anyone else was home, he wasn't about to show his face. My mom is a tall woman, much taller than I am. She towered over me, red-faced and frantic, fists clenched. Finally she got a grip and suggested we sit down at the kitchen table and talk like civilized people. I assured her I was the opposite of promiscuous, selective to a fault. My mom is not a crier, but she dabbed at her eyes, confessing her fear. She could not imagine what I was facing, the discrimination and perhaps the outright danger.

About a month later she made some private resolution. She joined our local chapter of PFLAG: Parents, Families, and Friends of Lesbians and Gays. At the medical center where she taught nursing, she put a pink triangle on her door. I told her people were going to think *she* was gay, but she said she didn't care.

"I want my students to know that I'm open-minded. I want them to know that if they need to talk, they can come to me."

After the advent of the Internet, she became an avid e-mailer, forwarding me information on Supreme Court decisions and various protests and marches in favor of gay rights. Much later, when gay marriage started becoming legal, she would forward me images her friends had sent, of the Statue of Liberty embracing Lady Justice, the first gay couple married in Massachusetts, and pretty much every other pro–gay rights picture that dropped into her in-box.

Somewhere during that time, I returned the promise ring to Johnny and told him the truth. He still worked at Lowe's, and I remember waiting for him in the parking lot one day. He came out untying his tie, then slipped it into his pocket. It struck me how much more mature he was than anyone else our age. He took the news surprisingly well, didn't say much other than the usual platitudes. Years later I was relieved to hear he'd married well, and had three beautiful children.

⌒

The only thing I felt committed to as my teen years were winding down was bodybuilding. I had stopped playing softball when I'd graduated from high school, and I'd lost my appetite for the extracurriculars at Hinds. I went to class and did my schoolwork without enthusiasm.

But I had discovered in myself a penchant for hard work. I found comfort in exerting myself, in the discipline of doing something taxing day after day. Pumping iron and bodybuilding required the kind of dedication and sustained focus that lit me up. I was always good at naming a goal and working toward its completion. I excelled at finishing what I started.

I began working out at a shabby old gym across from campus. It was almost all dudes and a lesbian or two. Weight lifters traditionally work in pairs, and I had teamed up with Randy. He was what today we would call a nerd. He had a studious look, tall and lanky, with long knobby-kneed legs and a chest that could use some developing, even by non-pumped-up standards. We committed to training twice a day, two hours in the morning, two in the afternoon. I was five foot two, weighed 104, and could bench-press 130. Every day, we just killed it.

I entered some bodybuilding contests, where I would compete in the lightweight category. When I moved on to the regional level, my mom, dad, and grandmom traveled with me. We'd drive in the station wagon, and after the event celebrate with pizza and beer. Alma wouldn't miss an event. If it had to do with me, there was no question that she was there. I could have been in the circus and she would come to watch me juggle. They were determined to support me, and in their minds I'm sure they thought it would be like watching me play softball, or perform during halftime with the Genteels.

The contests were all-day affairs. One competitor after the next would walk onstage in her swimsuit, suntanned and shiny with oil, and flex her muscles. My mom could hardly stand it. "Cathy! It's like watching paint dry," she would exclaim on the way home. My brothers rolled their eyes, thinking I was just on another kick.

The women I competed against were enormous, with deltoid muscles the size of grapefruits and pecs like the armor suit of a superhero; every leg muscle was a massive steel cable that could haul a barge. And oh the bulging veins, prized in the profession, but appalling to my mom, who knew a symptom of anabolic steroid use when she saw it.

I had never used steroids, but then one day Randy showed up to train and said he was going to get some and would I like to give them a try. Given the controversies that have since come to light in professional sports regarding steroid use, this must sound pretty bad. But this was the late 1980s, and steroids, at least in the South, where bodybuilding was king, were viewed as supplements, no more scandalous than amino acids or protein powder. Steroids were everywhere, and readily available. People chattered about them at the gym without a care, as if they were talking about what movie they'd seen over the weekend. They'd do a set of bench presses, disappear into the bathroom to plunge a needle into their thigh, then come out and hit it again.

Randy and I injected each other in the bathroom in our glutes, the top of that big butt muscle. We shot up before every workout. The effects on my body were instantaneous. Within a week my delts popped up, and I was sporting a six-pack. My voice, normally an average girly timbre, had fallen into the Demi Moore range.

One day not long after I'd started steroids, my mom walked in on me in the bathroom as I was getting out of the shower.

"Oh my gosh, what on earth are you doing?" she asked.

"What are you talking about?"

"You're taking steroids. I can tell. And you've got to stop."

I told her I would stop, but kept it up until the day I looked in the mirror and spied some facial hair.

⌒ six ⌒

After I quit bodybuilding, I found a new gym, an immaculate place that focused on overall fitness. There I met Blake, who was tall, blond, and bursting with energy. Everything I liked in a woman.

On our first date she brought along some freshly baked blueberry muffins. I found this to be incredibly sexy, a cute girl baking muffins just for me. I suspect I'm a little like a dude in that respect; the fastest way to my heart does indeed seem to be through my stomach.

We drove out to the Rez, the reservoir, sat on a picnic table, drank a few beers, and got to know each other. A big, bright moon shone down on the water, and we could easily watch the play of expressions on each other's faces. The night was warm and breezy and smelled of water and warm grass. We started to kiss, lightly at first, but soon we were splayed on top of the picnic table, dry-humping. We were forced to come up for air because a few trucks had pulled into the parking lot. That was the last thing we wanted—a truckload of rednecks gawking at us. So we did what any hot-and-bothered couple would do, ate another blueberry muffin.

Our romance went from zero to sixty in about three days. We were head-over-heels inseparable, a little crazy when forced to spend a single day apart.

Given what had happened with Jordan, I wasn't surprised when Blake confessed that she hadn't come out to her conservative family. Also, and equally unsurprising, before we fell in love she'd been dating a guy, a devout Christian named Edward. Mississippi is notably churchy; indeed, it's the most religious state in the nation, according to a number of reputable polls, and Edward was a Bible thumper of the first order.

Edward lived not far from my parents' house on Swan Lake Drive, and I'd run into him from time to time at the Jitney Jungle grocery. He was outgoing, salesmanlike, and perfectly cordial until the day Blake told him the truth, that she'd fallen in love with me. Edward began showing up at the gym when Blake and I worked out. We'd be side by side on the treadmills or at the weight machines and he would appear in his street clothes and lecture us. The music would be pounding, the machines whirring, and he'd yell, "Y'all are going straight to hell, you know that, right?"

We were polite. That's how both of us had been raised. At first Edward figured that as long as Blake hadn't "officially" come out, she was just being a willful and somewhat ridiculous sinner. He was her beard, a term with which I have no doubt Edward was unfamiliar.

Meanwhile, I'd enrolled at the University of Southern Mississippi at Hattiesburg, ninety miles south of Jackson, for the fall term. After two years at Hinds I still hadn't settled on a major, but I was closing in on twenty-one and knew it was time to dedicate myself more seriously to my education. My interest in food and nutrition, as well as sports and exercise, was a constant in my life, so I decided to major in exercise physiology.

One afternoon a few weeks before I was set to move to Hattiesburg, Blake met me at the gym at our usual time. I could see she was rattled. Her eyes were pink-rimmed from crying. We'd talked a lot about her moving with me to Southern Miss. She was several years older than me and had already graduated from college. She could get a job anywhere, and we were determined to be together. I wanted a steady girlfriend, a partner to come home to. I thought Blake was it, and Blake thought I was it, and that morning she'd summoned all her courage and came out to her parents and told Edward that she was breaking up with him for good. I knew it took a lot for her to do this, because it had taken a lot for me to do it—and my parents had been accepting.

We found ourselves two open exercise bikes side by side and hopped on. Blake said her parents went ballistic. She said they lost their minds. She said they never wanted her to see me again, and that they blamed me for turning her gay. She pedaled faster and faster. Her eyes shone, her tan cheeks flushed a deep rose. Then, out of the corner of my eye, I glimpsed the front door fling open, and someone stride inside furious with a sense of purpose.

It was Edward. From twenty paces I could see the rage in his eyes. He walked straight up to Blake and without pause pulled back his arm and punched her square in the face. She yowled, toppled off the bike and onto the rubber matting. I leapt off my bike and yelled, "What the hell!"

He stood over her and roared, "How dare you humiliate me!" His face was red. A vein on his forehead popped out. People came running, and someone appeared with a wad of wet paper towel, which Blake took and held against her swelling cheek. "You will not get away with humiliating me this way!" Then he turned and marched back out, his fists still in a ball.

After we ascertained that Blake was not grievously injured, Blake and I talked for hours. We were certain that holier-than-thou Edward giving his ex-girlfriend a black eye in front of a bunch of office workers reading *People* magazine on the treadmill was the last of it, and for several days all was quiet. It was August, the deep southern heat and humidity stupefying, even for us natives. We rode around town with the top down, counting the days until it was time to go.

Earlier in the summer I'd landed a part-time job at another gym across town. It was one of those gyms that put on airs, insisting their employees refer to it as a fitness center. When I showed up for my shift after The Incident, my boss summoned me into his office.

The moment he closed the door I knew I was in trouble. I racked my brain imagining what I could have done. I clocked in early and worked late, was clean and courteous, and in all ways was an exemplary employee. When he told me to sit across from his cheap desk I knew I was losing my job.

"I'm just going to ask you straight out, Cathy. We're hearing rumors that you're gay and that there was an altercation."

I told him what had happened, how Blake and I had been minding our own business working out at this other gym when Edward walked in and assaulted her. I used that word, *assault*, an actionable word by today's standards, but he swept it aside. "But are you with this woman?"

"Am I *with* this woman?"

"Women. Do you like women?"

I wish I could say that I spat out some sassy comeback or told him where he could shove it, but I just sat there and absorbed his disapproval. I knew how it was. In the eighties, in the South, people who associated with someone who was gay could be fired without cause. People who were gay—men or women—risked being beaten, even killed, with no police to protect you or lawyer to defend you. I kept my mouth shut,

eath the sink, I found the empty red and white con-
uffed at the bottom. I stared down at those smashed
s and knew we were doomed.

bed the cartons from the garbage and stuck them
: nose. I watched while she tried to formulate a lie,
uld hardly argue with the evidence. I flung the car-
e wall. She threw up her arms, as if she was afraid I
ottle her, which was not out of the realm of possibil-
furious at her, but more furious at myself.

emarkably, I made no move. Every day I went to
d I came home. I wanted hard proof of Blake's infi-
d I knew I had to bide my time.

ong after the Chinese food incident, on a Saturday
Blake hopped out of bed and said she was going to
big breakfast, but first needed to run to the store.
en thirty, early for a Saturday. I was only half awake
left. I went back to sleep, and when my eyes clicked
nine, and there was no smell of coffee brewing or
zling in the pan, or the rich, mouthwatering scent of
easy in butter, or any noise in the apartment at all, I
nough.

ler if Blake was so brazen because however betrayed
to feel, I never did anything about it. Or maybe it
use we had only one car. My Fiat was in the shop
. I had no means to come after her. I threw on some
d asked Natalie, a friend who was sleeping on the
ile between apartments, whether I could borrow the
er VW. We were chummy and generous in the way
students, and she tossed me the keys without asking
hen I would be back. I roared over to Julie's apart-
sure enough, Blake's car was parked in the driveway.
wed my boss at the fitness center in Jackson to talk

quashed the urge to point out that none of this drama had
happened here, at his fancy fitness center, and that it didn't
concern him in the slightest.

He didn't straight-out fire me, but it was decided that the
time had come for me to move on. I'd like to think I would
have fought a little more had I not been on the verge of giving
my notice anyway.

Blake and I moved into a small apartment in Hattiesburg
close to campus, and we were happy for a while. We threw
dinner parties and went out to eat with friends. New Orleans
was a mere one hundred miles south, and we liked to go there
on the weekends. Back then the legal drinking age in New
Orleans was eighteen, and I'd had years of party experience. I
knew all the good joints—jazz, drag, gay, straight, and strip.
I even knew a couple of voodoo shops. I knew where to get
the best oysters, pralines, beignets, po' boys, and muffuletta. I
knew who served the best hangover brunch, the coldest beer,
and the strongest drink. What sex shop had the best dildos at
the most reasonable price, and where you could score some
ecstasy. My own flirtation with X was mercifully short-lived.
I took it twice, liked it too much, and decided it'd be best if I
stuck to alcohol, which would prove to be more than enough
vice for me to handle.

It seemed that no sooner had we gotten truly settled—
flatware in the drawer, spoons and forks in the proper slots,
posters on the walls, every box unpacked—than Blake started
playing around. She was a great-looking blonde, tallish with
nice legs. That turns out to be a lot of people's type. Including
a she-devil named Julie, whom we'd met in New Orleans and
had hit on me first, and when I turned her down, moved on
to Blake.

I am nothing if not loyal. A devoted softball teammate,

drill squad member, student council member, sister, daughter, and granddaughter. Not too far in the future, I would become a loyal *commis, chef de partie,* sous-chef, and *chef de cuisine.* Even further down the road I would be a loyal and faithful wife. If I've said yes to you, if I've committed to you, I have your back no matter what. Despite the increase in our knock-down-drag-out arguments, I was loyal to Blake even when it was Blake out late with no real explanation; Blake trying out a new hairstyle; Blake buying new undergarments; Blake never there when I came home from class—from algebra, which I was flunking, because I was so consumed with the growing misery that was my relationship.

One late night, after too much Crown Royal and Diet Coke, I told her, "I know you're cheating. I haven't caught you yet, but I know I will."

Blake denied it, told me I was crazy and that she loved me, and I pretended to believe her. Even so, I started packing. I packed my books and pictures and made a stack of boxes against one wall, and there they sat for many months.

One weekend I went home and my mom and I were making dinner. It was dark outside, bright inside the kitchen, where there were no curtains on the windows, but thick shrubs provided privacy from the street. We had just opened a bottle of wine, an event that still signified an occasion in our house, and were laughing about something—no one likes to laugh more than my mom—happy to be together in the kitchen, as we always were. My mom was leaning against the counter, facing the window. Suddenly she shrieked and jumped. I whirled around to see Blake's face against the glass, peering in at us. My mom stomped outside and told her to get off the property, as if she were some crazy stranger. I didn't try to stop her.

Later, Blake would sob that she'd been seized by jealousy.

That she loved me so much she
with someone else, and when I
for the weekend, she'd smelled
conscience motivated this, of co
followed; she cried and begged
and eyed my cartons, yet did no

For my twenty-first birthda
make me a special dinner. Noth
pier. Even though I hadn't yet di
in my bones in the power of fo
mend rifts in a relationship and
that eating good food together v
filling your stomach. Food mark
birthdays, weddings, anniversa
Even the spread after a funeral i
of the person who's gone and
which revolves around making

I came home from class th
backpack slung off one shoul
inhaled to try to get a whiff of
apartment. When I cooked, the
oil infused the hallway outside
immediately that no feast was
lights on, and it smelled like V
down the counters.

But then Blake surprised me
with two plates piled high with

"You cooked?" I asked.

"Of course! It's your birth
cold."

I knew Hattiesburg take-ou
that night, when I went to thre

bage be
tainers
contain

I gra
under h
but she
tons at
might t
ity. I wa

Still,
school a
delity, a

Not
morning
cook us
It was se
when sh
open at
bacon si
eggs ove
thought

I wor
I claime
was beca
that wee
sweats a
couch w
keys to
of colleg
why or
ment and
I'd all

me into resigning because I was gay. I'd swallowed Blake's lies about her cheating and her cheap Chinese food. I was flunking algebra for the third time because I couldn't bring myself to keep asking, again and again, how to solve for x. But when I saw Blake's car, something fierce emerged in me.

I threw the door open and walked right in without knocking. They were in the kitchen, both wearing long T-shirts, the kind that double as nightgowns. Julie was sitting at her little kitchen table and Blake was standing, holding a cup of coffee. They looked as cozy as you please. The satiated just-been-fucked glow on their faces vanished when they saw me blow in like a Mississippi tornado.

"You"—I pointed my finger at Julie—"can have her. I'm done."

And with that I turned on my heel and left.

And this time I really was done. I drove back to the apartment and called my parents. "I need you guys to come down here now and help me move. Come as soon as possible. I'm leaving Blake and moving out today."

My mom said, "Hallelujah!" I could hear her, my dad, and Grandmom Alma doing the happy dance on the other end of the line. They made the ninety-mile trip in under an hour and a half. By this time Alma was in her eighties and was no stranger to the drama of human existence. As we were moving my cartons into the U-Haul, Blake came home and turned on the waterworks, begging me to stay. "Better back off," said Alma. "We're moving her out of here today whether you like it or not."

The saga continued for another year or so. Blake would follow me to class, crying and begging in front of students bustling around campus. She would show up at my apartment in the middle of the night and bang on the door. Once

I had to call the police. This being a southern story, there was an incident with a handgun, a small revolver that she carried in her purse. One hot Saturday afternoon I was studying at my kitchen table and received a call from Natalie, the friend who'd let me borrow her car to drive to Julie's that fateful day, and who now roomed with Blake. Natalie said Blake had been waving a pistol around and threatening to do herself in. I dropped everything and sped over, and as Natalie and I were standing in her living room, we heard a shot fired upstairs. Without thinking about whether Blake might shoot me, I flew up the steps three at a time to find Blake in her bedroom blubbering that I didn't love her anymore, and what was she going to do? She'd shot the light fixture, which had apparently satisfied her appetite for gun violence. She handed the gun over to me. After I sat her down and made sure she was all right, I got the hell out of there.

I dropped her revolver into my purse and forgot about it. A week later Natalie and I and a few guys she knew decided a bar crawl was in order. It may have been after exams. We drank at home, then hopped into the car and sped down the dark highway in search of a great bar someone knew down in Purvis, or maybe Lumberton. The radio was cranked, windows rolled down, we were hollering and singing into the night. Then, the red and blues started flashing behind us. We weren't especially panic stricken, not at first. Your average Mississippi cop was unmoved in the face of an open beer. Usually they'd sidle over to the window and say, "I'll just take that beer from you and give you this ticket. Now don't let me catch you again and get on home."

But this particular officer pulled the driver out of the car, and without any cordial chitchat handcuffed him and tossed him into the back of his patrol car. Natalie and I were in the backseat clinging to each other, drunk and sobbing. "We're going to jail! Some crazy backwater jail where we're going to get raped and murdered." We were scared, but it wasn't until I remembered the pistol in my purse that I saw spots before my eyes and felt my internal organs clench with fear.

The cop found the gun and took us all back to the station. I was sobering up quick and thought with horror of how my parents and Grandmom would react. They would be disappointed, sad, and pissed, and not necessarily in that order. I thought about their utter devotion to me, their commitment to helping me get through school, the way they dropped everything and probably broke a few speed limits themselves racing down to Hattiesburg to help me move. They really didn't deserve this.

I was handcuffed, fingerprinted, and booked for carrying a concealed weapon. I explained that the reason I had the gun was that I'd taken it away from a friend who'd threatened to kill herself. I offered to show them how I didn't even know how to shoot the thing. I said I was happy and relieved that they had confiscated it. I was smart enough to keep saying *a friend* and not *my girlfriend.* I would probably still be in jail had I dropped that bomb on those good old boys.

They confiscated the pistol, issued me a fine, and released me.

Not long after that, I found out that I'd finally passed algebra.

~ seven ~

My mom kept a scrapbook for each of her kids, and on the inside of mine, written on the bottom left corner of the front cover in black permanent marker, it said: Born April 3, 1967. Adopted April 10, 1967. The large, clear hand proclaims there are no secrets here. My parents made a point of treating my adoption, and also the adoption of my brother Mike, as if they were the most normal family events.

Then as now, adoption is closed in Mississippi, but when I turned twenty-one I was given the chance to find my birth mother. I'd wondered about her, of course, but at that moment all I really knew was that I came from good, healthy stock. A few years earlier, when I was around eighteen, I became curious about my health history. I can't remember why I was so curious, other than I was beginning to understand that I didn't share my parents' DNA, but had the DNA of other people who might be wandering the earth with some inheritable syndrome or disease that I should know about. I'd asked my parents, and they said all they knew was that the Mississippi Children's Home had given me a clean bill of health before my adoption was finalized.

What I didn't know was that my question inspired my mom to contact the Children's Home. She learned that my birth mother called the home every year around my birthday, hoping to be in touch with me. My mom then wrote my birth mother a letter, telling her in general terms about my upbringing, how she was a nurse and my father was a teacher, and how I was a good student and fine athlete. Not strictly true, but my mom was generally proud of me. My birth mother wrote right back and said she was married with two kids, and that whenever I was ready she would love to meet me. It turned out that she was also a registered nurse, just like Mom.

On the night of my birthday dinner we stuffed ourselves with *kota kapama* and Alma's cheesecake. It being my birthday, I went for that second slice. I remember my mom going from room to room opening windows, letting in the smell of spring. The dogwoods were blooming, as well as the saucer magnolias with their fragrance of overripe citrus.

She returned from the other room with a stack of letters. "Cathy," she said, "when you had those questions about your birth mom awhile back we contacted her. I kept a copy of what I wrote, and here's what she wrote back. Also, we thought you should know that she called and wanted to meet you when you turned eighteen, but we felt it was too soon."

"Too soon? I was eighteen! A legal adult." I felt a swirl of conflicting emotions at the thought of meeting the woman who gave birth to me, but my kneejerk response was to get het up and offended. I was irked that Mom and Dad contacted her and hadn't told me. "You were coping with a lot of serious issues then," said my mom. "Adding another issue to the mix was the last thing you needed then. When she called asking again last week, we thought it was time. If you want to meet her it's okay with us. We're with you all the way."

Along with the recent letters was a stack of envelopes. Every year on my birthday, Joanne—my birth mother—had written to the home, asking after me, and these were those letters. I took each one out of its white envelope and read it. The same handwriting, year after year, wondering the same thing: How was I doing? Was I healthy? Happy? Well loved? I was a little teary-eyed. I felt both stunned and special. All these letters. I marveled at her determination and suspected I inherited my penchant for stubborn loyalty from her, for which I suddenly felt unaccountably grateful.

The next morning, while my dad was getting ready to leave for work and my mom was scrambling up some eggs, I told her I wanted to call my birth mother. Right that minute. She slid the eggs onto a plate, picked up the phone, and made the call. A week later my parents, Grandmom, and I were on our way to the Mississippi Children's Home to meet Joanne. I was so eager to lay eyes on the woman who'd given me life.

A social worker greeted us in the waiting area. She put my mom, dad, and Alma in one room and me in another. There, the social worker and I waited for my birth mother. I believe I would have been more nervous if it hadn't been so surreal. I had a mother and father whom I loved beyond measure, and yet now I would have another mother, one whose DNA I shared. The door opened and Joanne walked in, and we fell into each other's arms. The Coras were tall people—Dad is six feet and my mom is five eight. I'm five two, and Joanne was petite like me. I looked so much like her. She had fine, dark features and small hands that I recognized. The nail beds, the tapering fingers, all like mine. Years later, after we'd spent some time together, we would marvel at all the mannerisms we shared, the way we gestured when we talked and the way we laughed.

We hugged until it got awkward, then both laughed and blotted the tears from our eyes.

The social worker sat on a metal chair off to the side. She was there to help facilitate the conversation, but her services were unnecessary. We talked easily, and Joanne had twenty-plus years' worth of things to tell me.

Joanne was fifteen when she went to a concert with a friend and fell hard for the drummer in one of the bands. His name was Knox, and he was twenty, an older man. He had long hair that hung over one eye. When she wound up pregnant, his daddy told her daddy that marrying her was out of the question, that it would ruin his life. It was 1966, and her options were to have an illegal abortion, to have the baby and keep it, or to have the baby and put it up for adoption. She knew a girl who'd snuck away to New York for an abortion, but her parents were God-fearing Mississippi Christians and no way no how was this ever going to happen.

She was packed off to a foster home before she was even showing. Her foster parents were an old couple and business was so good they built an addition onto the back of their house specifically to house their foster children. The old man liked to wander back and look through the bathroom window and watch her while she bathed. When she told her parents about this, they sent her to the unwed mothers' home in New Orleans. The first day she was there she was on the trolley by herself and a man exposed himself to her; she was immediately whisked off to the Florence Crittenton Home, where she met girls from California and New York. She liked her roommate, a teacher from up north who had her baby only a few days before I was born.

Joanne told me that she had the option not to see me, and even though she knew it would bring her heartbreak she had to hold me, count my fingers and toes, and look into my eyes. She passed me over to the Mississippi Children's Home, and then she went home herself, to Greenwood. She was sixteen.

Still, a month later she took the bus back to Jackson, then a taxi to the Children's Home. She marched in, shaking with the nerve of what she was about to do, and asked to have me back. She thought that if she walked in the door of her parents' house with a babe in arms, they would glimpse their own flesh and blood and experience a change of heart. But she was too late; I had already been placed with Spiro and Virginia Lee Cora.

She didn't believe them. "You're lying!" she screamed. "I know she's back there. Let me see her. Let me have her back." She was hysterical. No one could calm her down. The woman at the front desk called Joanne's dad. Joanne's mom had reported her missing earlier in the day, and had had a pretty good idea where she was headed.

"Every year on your birthday I would call the Children's Home and ask whether you were okay. They couldn't tell me anything other than that you were alive. Once I sent a doll, but I'm not sure whether you ever got it. I've spent a lifetime looking for you. I knew that if I glimpsed you in another woman's arms or in a stroller, or playing with a bunch of kids at the park, or even later, hanging out at the mall, that I would absolutely recognize you."

Only a few years earlier, Gaylon, a friend of hers, spied a picture of the new crop of Gayfer Girls on the department store wall near customer service. Thinking she recognized me, she called Joanne, who rushed over to see for herself. "I knew it was you," she told me. "I didn't even need to see your birthmark." I smiled at that old southern saying, which means *I know you so well I would recognize you anywhere.*

I felt dizzy trying to absorb the reality of this—that while I'd been going about my business growing from child to teen to young adult, the woman who'd given birth to me was looking into the faces of all the girls she came upon on the street, seeing if it was me, her daughter.

After our reunion, Joanne and I saw each other a lot. We met for lunch, and sometimes she came to dinner at our home on Swan Lake Drive. Once she invited me to drive up to the small town of Belzoni, in the Delta, to the house where my birth father, Knox, lived. Belzoni, population two thousand, give or take, is famous for its farm-raised catfish and is home of the World Catfish Festival, held every year in April. I thought of Knox only as Joanne's baby daddy. He hadn't taken responsibility for having created a child. I couldn't think of him as my birth father. I knew exactly who my daddy was, and it wasn't this guy.

Knox didn't live there anymore. After college he'd moved to the Caribbean, where he started a charter boat business. Still, she wanted me to see where he grew up. She was hoping we could meet; she at least wanted me to clap eyes on him.

When we arrived, his mother was outside mowing the lawn in shorts and a sleeveless plaid shirt.

"Who're you?" his mother asked.

"Joanne. Knox's daughter Cathy is in the car."

The woman just stared, didn't say a word.

"She would at least like to see a picture of her daddy," said Joanne.

The woman dropped the mower handle and went into the house. She came back with a single snapshot and said, "When you get through leave it on the porch. Then please leave."

I watched her in disbelief. Was this a joke? Joanne's family had been eager and happy to get to know me and embrace me as one of their own. How could this woman not appreciate that I was her son's flesh and blood, *her* flesh and blood? I stared at her, this old country woman who looked to be about a hundred, perched on her skinny legs, a cigarette stuck on her lip, and I thought, *You are as mean as a snake.*

As far as I know, her son still lives in the Caribbean. Through an old high school friend, Joanne discovered that he eventually married and had two children, a boy and a girl, now college aged, my half siblings. He apparently knows about me, and knows I know about him, but there it rests.

My parents encouraged me to spend as much time with Joanne as I wished. Now that I'm a mother myself, I often wonder how much discipline this required, and the strength and selflessness it must have taken for them to let go. They were confident and had complete faith in the love I had for them, and they for me, and in our bond, so that I could build a relationship with Joanne. It's a testament to the grace and courage of my parents.

I could tell my mom worried a bit that Joanne, eager to catch up on all those lost years, might overwhelm me with her need to develop a relationship. Joanne was keen not just on spending time together but on drawing me into the life of her mother and sisters.

One day my mom sat me down and said, "Honey, if you don't want to get this involved you can blame us, just say, 'I don't think my parents would care for me to do that.'" I wanted to get to know her, but it was complicated to try to negotiate the emotional terrain. I needed time to adjust. This had the potential to be a deep, important relationship, but I was only twenty-one. I didn't even know myself.

When my twenty-second birthday rolled around, my parents invited Joanne and her family to the party. Taki and Maria came. Before the party I sat my parents down on the couch and said, "Look, Joanne may be my birth mom, but y'all are my parents." I loved having Joanne in my life, but I wanted to be sure my mom and dad knew I had room in my heart for them all.

This wasn't just a Hallmark sentiment. Joanne and my parents seemed to understand intuitively that the best way to show their love and support for their daughter was to form a united front. This was progressive thinking twenty-five years ago. The notion that I would not just find and grow to love my birth mother, but that she and my parents would form a relationship, was extraordinary. I like to think of it as kismet. Both Joanne and my mom were nurses. My mom's birthday is September 14, and Joanne's is September 18.

Over the years I've also gained an extended family through Joanne: a birth grandmother, Jessie; two aunts, Judy and Jan; an uncle, Webb; a half brother, Jason; a half sister, Kim; a niece, and a bushel of nephews. Joanne and her husband, Terrie, live a mere twenty minutes from Swan Lake Drive; to this day, whenever I find myself in Jackson we all get together. I call Joanne every Sunday, just as I do my mom. I never forget how lucky I am.

⌒ eight ⌒

I knew I loved food, and I knew that cooking made me feel settled and happy, but otherwise it wasn't obvious that I'd make a life for myself in the culinary world. I was female, for one thing, and in the early 1990s female chefs were about as plentiful as female fighter pilots.

My Wikipedia entry amusingly reads: "After receiving her bachelor of science degree in exercise physiology and biology at the University of Southern Mississippi, she enrolled at the Culinary Institute of America in Hyde Park, New York." It's not untrue, but makes the journey sound so straightforward, as though I sashayed through my graduation in Hattiesburg in the sweltering June heat one day, then packed up my knives and sped on up to Hyde Park the next.

But real life provides very few clear-cut aha moments. And there was no moment of clarity or clear turning point when I knew I'd make a life in the kitchen. I struggled to figure out what to do with my life.

My mom and dad had gotten up at dawn and gone to work every day. They had taken second jobs and weekend shifts and earned extra college degrees, and still, I couldn't quite figure out what adults did all day. Or, better put, what I was supposed to do all day, now that I had a college degree. I moved back in with my parents, a boomerang child before the term became popular.

It occurred to me that I could prolong my existential dilemma a bit longer by spending the summer backpacking around Europe. I'd been to Texas and a few other southern states, but otherwise I was undertraveled. My parents weren't opposed, but they were not about to foot the bill, so I got a job.

I had never worked in a real restaurant, but I have a habit of going big when I set my mind to something. So, without a lick of experience, I somehow landed a job at what was at the time the top restaurant in town, a white-tablecloth place on State Street in downtown Jackson, not far from the Old Capitol Building. I began as a waitress, but also worked as a cocktail waitress and then bartender. But during slow times I always found myself wandering back into the kitchen. I loved to cook at home, but the chefs and cooks were clearly up to something very different. It seemed as if they were doing ten things at once, with confidence and an air of nonchalance. The plates of food they produced were as beautiful as they were delicious. At home I followed recipes—one of my all-time favorite cookbooks had been the classic spiral-bound, red-and-white-checked Betty Crocker—but these guys, and they were *all* guys, held all the information they needed in their heads. I was both impressed and intrigued and thought how great it would be to have all those skills at your disposal.

As I was learning to serve food, my personal life took on a grounded feeling I'd never known to that point. My mom had finished her PhD program and had returned to Swan Lake Drive. Alma, who was getting up there in years, had grown accustomed to living with us, and stayed on in her floral-wallpapered bedroom. She kept right on doing our laundry and turning out her spectacular desserts. Joanne, my birth mother, was a regular part of my life. Then I met Hannah.

I was twenty-three, and in the four years since I'd come out, Jackson had opened a few more gay bars. One night some friends and I found ourselves at a place called—I kid you not—Carpet World. I started chatting with a cute blond girl at the bar only to learn after twenty concentrated minutes of flashing my smile and fluttering my lashes that she was straight. She in turn introduced me to Hannah, who to my great surprise was dressed in the outfit of the hard-core Pentecostal holy roller: knee-length skirt, cotton blouse with Peter Pan collar, and a long braid down her back.

What on earth was a Pentecostal girl doing in a gay bar? My family was Greek Orthodox, and active in the church community. We were churchgoers, as many good southerners are, but as I was to learn, Hannah's people were fervent, Bible-thumping Pentecostals, the type who spoke in tongues and practiced the laying on of hands. She'd spent her formative years in a trailer park in Slidell, Louisiana, a small town on the north shore of Lake Pontchartrain, with her parents and three sisters. Hannah moved to Jackson to live with her grandmother when she was in elementary school, and after she graduated from high school she got a job working for Allstate insurance company. She stayed with her grandma, and the thing that I found fascinating was that even though her people routinely damned her to hell for her sexual orientation, she just took it in stride.

Her parents begged her to talk to their pastor, and practically gave themselves hernias praying for her, but she would just smile and say no, thanks. I was impressed that she could stand her ground and be kind to her detractors at the same time.

It wasn't love at first sight, but we grew into an easy friendship and eventually something more. We hung out with the same group of women, and often at the end of a party, or a night at a club, we would wind up together talking. Hannah was always the designated driver, and I always seemed to have my eye on her hot, straight best friend. One night I noticed that she'd cut her braid, had replaced her skirts with tight jeans, and was wearing mascara and lipstick. I saw she was pretty, with expressive eyes and a lovely smile.

New Orleans became our stomping grounds. Especially because after a night on the town we could crash at Hannah's family's place. Slidell was a mere thirty minutes from the city, over the I-10 Twin Span bridge, a trip that was always fueled by a peach daiquiri, extra shot, from one of Louisiana's roadside drive-thru daiquiri shops.

We had our favorite gay bars, where I would usually try to pick up a hot little Dixie chick and Hannah would function as my wingman. She wasn't happy seeing me with other girls, and would try to hook up herself, but without much success. After a night on the town there was usually a scene, with Hannah in tears and me racked with guilt, heartache all around. Eventually, Hannah tired of waiting for me and started seeing someone else. That got my attention real quick, and my feelings for her began to change.

I wish I could say that I saw her inner beauty before she started wearing lip gloss and curling her hair, but the truth is that only after her transformation did I realize maybe Hannah and I could be more than friends. Since the night we'd met she'd made no secret of her attraction to me, but over time I came to realize that I had someone special right under my nose, someone who loved me and would have my back.

Hannah, sweet and easygoing, was game for anything. Once I'd saved enough money, she thought nothing of quitting her job at Allstate and taking off for Europe for twelve weeks. Our itinerary was based on the places I'd dreamed about as a girl, lying on my belly on the living room floor, perusing my dad's atlas: England and France, Spain and Portugal, Amsterdam, Switzerland and Germany, Italy and, of course, Greece.

We were on a strict budget, staying in youth hostels and one-star hotels. We purchased a Eurail pass and sometimes took an overnight train to save money. We ate the local bread, cheese, cured meat, and wine. If we ate out, it was usually street food. We dutifully phoned home once a week, but otherwise we were completely on our own. We were twenty-three. We traveled well together, a pair of pretty young things abroad, reveling in our adventures, which included not one but two incidents involving flashers—once in Naples and once in Saint-Tropez—and a misadventure that occurred on the train from Spain to Portugal.

Our Eurail pass was only good for economy class. It was mid-July and murderously hot. We sat in the last car with the train windows thrown open, dust, pollen, and flies circulating throughout the car. Hannah and I were tired and cranky. We bickered over something I've long since forgotten. I thought we could use a break and went to the bar car, where I ordered a sandwich and a cold beer. I struck up a conversation with a Spanish soldier. We passed the time nursing our beers. In those days there were no bullet trains, and our train lumbered across the countryside, stopping at every small station along the way. Eventually there came an announcement that we were reaching Lisbon, and I bid him farewell and started back to my seat at the back of the train. Except there *was* no back of the train. Somewhere along the route the train had been decoupled, and Hannah and all my stuff were gone.

I sprinted back through the cars to find the Spanish soldier before he disappeared. Sweat poured down the side of my face and I could feel my pulse beating in my throat. I caught up with him, grabbed him, and told him what happened. He was unruffled, got off the train with me at the next stop, explained my predicament to the person in the ticket booth, and soon I was back on a train headed in the opposite direction. I was so relieved after having been so frantic that I bought myself another beer, stuck my head out the train window like a happy retriever, and enjoyed the ride all the way back.

When we reached the station, I spied Hannah on the platform with a policeman. I could see she had been crying, and I waved out the window, happy that I'd been so quick on my feet and solved the problem easily. Hannah was relieved to see me, but also wanted to bean me for getting us into this predicament in the first place.

The high point of the trip was our pilgrimage to Skopelos, Greece, the island of my ancestors. I felt like a southern girl through and through, but part of me was always aware that my dad's side of the family was Greek. And not simply Greek immigrants who'd made their way from the Old Country to become Greek Americans who ran restaurants in Mississippi, but also mysterious and exotic aunts, uncles, and cousins who were born and died on the same small island in the Aegean.

Before Hannah and I had left, my dad arose in the predawn dark to make phone calls to Skopelos to arrange our visit. I remember awaking in the dark to hear him down the hall, speaking Greek to strangers who were not strangers at all, but family. The mere thought of it thrilled me to the core. Due east of the Pelion peninsula, the drumstick-shaped island of Skopelos is a mere thirty-seven square miles of mountainous terrain covered in pine and oak, and dotted with plum and almond orchards. Karagiozoses have lived here for centuries, in a house on a hillside that my aunts, uncles, and cousins called "grandfather's house," a modest white structure with a table outside beneath the olive trees, overlooking the blue-green sea.

When we arrived, my dad's cousin's wife, whom everyone called Aunt Demetra, had a spread waiting, the rustic table laid end to end with white platters of homemade bread, tangy tzatziki, spicy feta spread, artichoke hearts braised in lemon juice, and buttery, light spanakopita stuffed with fresh spinach and the most flavorful feta I'd ever eaten. Demetra was worried we were starving. Even though she spoke very little English, I watched her wring her hands a little, then she opened her palms toward a pair of wobbly chairs. She pushed the platters toward us, nodded, and smiled. Although we'd had breakfast before we'd boarded the ferry in Thessaloníki only a few hours before, we dug in. Without speaking the same language, our mutual happiness was apparent.

The next day we were introduced to my great-aunt Eleni, Dad's uncle John's wife, who lived in a tiny apartment overlooking the harbor, the best spot on the island. She brought us thick Greek coffee made in a briki pot and served with a spoon sweet—a thick dollop of syrupy fruit preserves—a traditional gesture of Greek hospitality. Maybe it was because we were tired of cheap hotels, cheap meals, and the general stresses of travel, but Aunt Eleni's coffee and sweets, simple as they were, restored us. We felt nourished and cared for. Hannah and I stayed on Skopelos for only a few days, but it was long enough for me to glimpse something simple and profound: that the joy and satisfaction of making and sharing food, whether you are cooking and serving or receiving and enjoying, are universal. The passion my Greek relatives put into their food and the passion my southern family put into *their* food was the same. Good food, served with care, had the power to connect even people who didn't speak the same language. I was so moved by this that I felt a goal begin to materialize. Since I'd graduated from college I'd felt at loose ends, but on the long flight home I kept coming back to the same idea, that I might be able to make a living cooking, providing this kind of experience for others.

⌒

After Hannah and I returned to the States I got a job at Amerigo, a casual Italian establishment on Old Canton Road not far from the country club. They served what passed as authentic Italian in Jackson: scampi, lasagna, pasta pomodoro, and spaghetti in a traditional red sauce with a jumbo meatball. I waited tables for a while, and when there was an opening for a cook, I put in for it.

Ideas kept me up at night. For a few fevered weeks, Hannah and I explored financing the purchase of Walker's Drive-In in the arty Fondren district. It was classic Jackson, a modest box diner with a peony-pink neon sign, aqua front door with a pair of classic Art Deco portholes, and a lot of potential. It could not have been a bigger pipe dream, but my instinct about the place was flawless. James Beard Award finalist Derek Emerson would one day buy it and turn it into one of the coolest joints in Jackson.

Then we hatched a plan to open Jackson's first Caribbean restaurant. Hannah drew up a business plan and I wrote the menus. I imagined curries and jerk shrimp, mango salsas, fried ripe plantains. For a solid month, after I got off my shift at

Amerigo, I'd come home and shower, rinsing off the smells of olive oil, garlic, and oregano, and start my second shift, devising jerk rubs and experimenting with fruity Caribbean salsas. I fried up plantains and invited Taki and Maria over. I made jerk chicken skewers with brown sugar, soy sauce, and thyme. I added pineapple, red peppers, and jalapeños to the rub. Hannah and I put on our best outfits and met with local businessmen who'd invested in other restaurants, and also some investors Taki knew. They found our fevered ambition amusing, and every last one said no.

I remained weirdly undaunted. I should have been discouraged. It was now 1992 and the number of female restaurant owner-chefs I knew were exactly none. Certainly there were none in the South. I'd heard of Julia Child and Alice Waters, who wasn't even *Alice Waters* yet, but merely the owner of the popular, upscale hippie bistro Chez Panisse. That was it. Like Marine Corps sniper, drag queen, and pope, executive chef was apparently a job only for men. Ironic, because many of the most bad-ass home cooks I knew were women, and the best, most-cherished recipes of most of the male cooks I know all came from their grannies.

Amerigo was my first cooking job. There I learned the steps of food prep, how to butcher meat and clean fish, and how to make basic sauces. Taki had introduced me to the art of sautéing, and now I got to practice it every day. After I had been there for about four months, a cooking competition called Taste of Elegance came to Jackson.

The kitchen manager at Amerigo, a jovial tweaker named Buddy, was hot to enter the contest and asked me to be his sous chef. I was competitive by nature and loved the idea of a contest, so I said yes. We met a few times about six weeks before the competition, but it was apparent from the beginning that we weren't going to be able to make it work. He had a vision of a dish featuring venison sausage that sounded revolting, and he wasn't open to any of my suggestions, so we parted ways.

Before I teamed up with Buddy, I'd had no intention of entering the contest on my own. I'd been working in the culinary world for a whopping four months, and some of the other chefs who were entering, among the best in Mississippi, had decades of experience. But now that he'd cut me loose I was determined to enter. Why not? What did I have to lose?

One of the things I'd noticed at my aunt's table in Greece was that her simple yet spectacular food was made using mostly local ingredients. In 2015 we take this philosophy for granted, but in the early 1990s the idea of using indigenous food in season was unheard of. If you could get blueberries grown in another hemisphere in the dead of winter, there was no reason not to make pie.

I decided to see what I could do with traditional southern ingredients that my family and friends loved—pork loin, crawfish, and pecans. My dish evolved as I practiced cooking the various elements. Every night after work I came home and cooked; sometimes I didn't get started until midnight. While my family slept I would practice roasting pork loin, trying to figure out the perfect temperature and cooking time, so that it would be juicy but not pink. I wanted to make a champagne beurre blanc sauce, and polished Julia Child's recipe from *Mastering the Art of French Cooking*. I must have made it a half dozen times, striving to ensure it wasn't too oily and didn't break. I didn't know quite what to do with the pecans: toast them and sprinkle them on top? Add them to the beautiful pale yellow champagne beurre blanc?

The contest was held in a conference room at the big Mississippi Trade Mart, part of the state fairgrounds complex. We prepped our dishes in our home kitchens, then cooked on site.

I settled on a spinach-and-crawfish-stuffed pork loin with champagne toasted pecan butter sauce, and only after I plated my entry did I learn the judge was one of the most famous chefs in the nation, and easily one of the most respected chefs in the South—the great Paul Prudhomme.

There were only a few genuine celebrity chefs then. James Beard and Julia Child were perhaps the best known, followed closely by Prudhomme, the man who'd pretty much single-handedly popularized Cajun and Creole cooking. Upon learning the identity of the judge, my confidence deflated like a balloon. My dish featured ingredients near to his heart. I surmised that either that would make my dish more appealing, or he would judge me more harshly.

I was the only female chef in the competition. Together with the other nine male chefs, we brought our dishes to a long table where Prudhomme would conduct a blind taste test. Buddy was there with his venison sausage. He smirked when he noticed me. I ignored him, told myself that even though I didn't have a chance, it was good practice.

We were ushered into another room to wait while Prudhomme and the other judges deliberated. I sat and amused myself, adding up the combined years of cooking experience my competitors boasted; I came up with over a century. We were called back in and stood in a long row, our hands clasped behind our backs. Prudhomme and one of the organizers walked toward my end of the line, and suddenly a medal hung on a thick red, white, and blue ribbon was being draped around my neck. I was so shocked. I thought this must be some runner-up prize, some thanks-for-playing award. But no, I had won.

My picture appeared in the *Clarion-Ledger*. In my chef whites, the medal hanging around my neck, a big grin on my face, I presented my winning plate to the camera.

⌒

Winning the Taste of Elegance confirmed that I was on the right path, but nothing changed for a while. Paul Prudhomme didn't call me the next day and beg me to come and work for him. I went to work, then came home and tried to re-create the specials of the day. I got obsessed for a bit with perfecting roast chicken, a simple dish that can be the most delicious thing you've ever tasted or dry and completely depressing. I must have been about eighteen chickens into the process when I opened the paper one morning and saw an ad for a book-signing that night down in Natchez, a two-hour drive. Julia Child was coming with her new cookbook, *The Way to Cook*.

I worshipped Julia Child. My brother Chris and I had watched *The French Chef* when we were kids. I always thought Chris might become a chef. He worshipped Justin Wilson, the "cooking Cajun," and walked around saying, "I gar-on-tee it's good!" My parents had given me both volumes of *Mastering* on consecutive Christmases, and I studied them as if they were sacred texts. Like so many other people, both home cooks and aspiring professionals, I felt a special affinity with Julia. I had a hunch that if I could just ask her advice about how I should proceed, she would be able to help me chart my future course.

I told my mom and grandmom to drop what they were doing and cancel their afternoon plans, we were going on a road trip. They obliged—a testament to how supportive my family was, the degree to which they got on board whenever I got a wild hair. Which was fairly frequently.

We arrived at the book signing in plenty of time, but the line was out the door. I'd once read in a magazine article that Julia traveled with a minder. She was one of those people who was truly interested in others, and the fear was that Julia would fall into conversation with the first person in line to have her book signed. The minder kept the line moving.

Julia was a few months from her eightieth birthday, but she had the energy of a woman decades younger. As the line dwindled I watched the grace with which she greeted her fans. I felt sure that if her minder didn't rush me along, she would speak to me.

After the last person had closed her newly signed book, thanked Julia, and moved off, Julia capped her pen and straightened up. I placed myself in front of her.

"Mrs. Child," I began. Then whatever smooth speech I had prepared about myself and my ambitions evaporated. "I want to cook."

She sized me up, then without hesitation said, "Then you must go to school. The Culinary Institute of America is the Harvard of culinary schools. Make it your number one." Julia warmed to the subject and went on about the joys and tribulations I'd face if I chose this life path. Her minder looked at her watch at least a dozen times, but Julia was on a roll. She encouraged me, saying the culinary life was the best life there was, but also warned me that it was brutal and competitive. "It's a man's world," she said. "You must know this. But be stubborn and intractable in your determination and success will be inevitable."

The next morning, swooning with optimism, I called the Culinary Institute of America for an application.

⟶ nine ⟿

I was twenty-six years old when I loaded up my car and drove north to Hyde Park, New York. The Fiat was a memory, and now I drove a more sensible Honda that Grandmom gave me when she was no longer able to drive. I was fired up. My inspirational conversation with the great Julia Child fueled me as I made my application then settled in to wait. I knew I didn't quite meet the requirements, which were stricter then than they are now. My college GPA was good, but they also liked you to have at least a year of experience cooking professionally. I was short a few months, but I hoped that winning the Taste of Elegance would make up for it.

When I received my acceptance, I was only marginally surprised. I felt like I was on a roll. My life had truly begun! I dutifully hassled with the student loan people, then braced myself to talk through the situation with Hannah. We had been together about two and a half years by then, and I was well aware that I often took advantage of her laid-back nature. I didn't want her to break up with me, but I also knew it was a lot to ask her to agree to a long-distance relationship. She was unfazed by my decision, and believed in my future as a chef wholeheartedly. "*Go*," she said. "Do what you have to do, and I'll be waiting for you when you get back."

The Culinary Institute of America was twelve hundred

miles away from Swan Lake Drive. As I drove across Alabama and Tennessee, then up through Virginia, Maryland, and Pennsylvania, it occurred to me that I had never been north. I had lived in Mississippi my entire life, and the few times I'd traveled, it had either been west to Texarkana, or to Europe. I didn't think it would make much difference. I'd never understood how vast and diverse our country truly is.

Hyde Park struck me at first glance as cold and formal, the light silvery and sad. The air didn't smell like dry grass and magnolia blossoms, but like something industrial. The Culinary Institute was housed in a former Jesuit seminary on the banks of the Hudson River, a huge brick building with white columns. A lot of people found it elegant and stately, but I thought it was imposing and unnerving. I knew I would be living in a dorm, but once I was standing in the middle of my room with its twin bed, four-drawer dresser, desk, and chair, I was filled with misgivings. Had I actually signed up for this? The last and only time I'd lived in a dorm was my first semester at Hinds Community College with Sandy, when half the time I was drunk, but at least it was with my best friend. Now I was halfway across America in another crappy little room, in the company of strangers.

But there was little time to think that first week, a blur of tours, orientation sessions, including a stern lecture on the history of the uniform and toqueing ceremony, the issuing of the culinary tool kit and pastry tool kit, more lectures on how we were supposed to be immaculate every moment of every day, and would get points deducted if our whites were not spotless. I didn't know a soul, not even a friend of a friend of a friend, and no one seemed interested in getting acquainted.

My enduring memory of this time is how out of place I felt, how lame and clueless. I could sit in my dorm room all by myself and make myself blush to the tips of my hair remembering how proud I'd felt winning the Taste of Elegance with my stuffed pork loins. In class, it was obvious to everyone that I was inexperienced and unprepared. I was terrified at the thought of how much I didn't know. I could make a few tasty dishes in my mother's kitchen, but otherwise I was ignorant. In Jackson we had parsley, and once my mom tried to grow oregano in the backyard, but most of my fellow students already knew how to make a *sachet d'épices*, a little cheesecloth pouch filled with herbs and spices, usually bay leaf, thyme, parsley stems, garlic, and whole black peppercorns, used to enhance the flavor of stocks. I hadn't even heard of it.

I'd never been aware that I had what some folks might consider a thick southern accent, but my instructors had a hard time understanding me. Most of my fellow students were nineteen or twenty, and struck me as squirrely and young. The sopping, mosquito-slapping Mississippi heat was nothing to me, but in Hyde Park I was always cold. It was pure misery from sunrise to midnight, which were the hours they expected you to keep.

Two weeks into the semester I went into the administration office and withdrew, hurled my crap back into my Honda, and drove home, eighteen hours straight through. The Culinary Institute refunded my tuition and fees, no questions asked. Their decency made me feel even more like a failure than I already did, which I didn't think was possible.

Although she was too tactful to say it, I'm sure Hannah was happy to see me for about seventeen minutes, after which my self-pity and wallowing must have been insufferable. I had had some dark days, but these had to have been the darkest. What in the hell was I doing? I had wasted forty-five minutes of the great Julia Child's time, and at her age that was a lot.

I had disappointed my parents and grandmom, who never scoffed at my enthusiasm and thought I had it in me to be a great chef. I had prepared Hannah for a long-distance relationship, only to show up back on her doorstep (actually my doorstep, since she was living with my parents and grandmom on Swan Lake Drive), a coward and a quitter.

What had I done? In those days, every top restaurant insisted on staffing its kitchen with graduates from the Culinary Institute of America. Every newspaper ad began: "Looking for CIA grad." Closing the door on an education at the Culinary Institute meant closing the door on a life as a chef. Period. Things are more relaxed today. Restaurants would prefer their cooks to have some cooking school experience, but it's no longer a prerequisite. Still, for me, a girl from Mississippi, education would always be my ticket out. I valued the importance of it then and still do.

Also, even though I was in the middle of a meltdown during my short time there, I saw clearly that for me to succeed in the larger world, I would need to make friends and connections with people from New York, at the time the undisputed fine-dining capital of the nation. The whole experience had emphasized the fact that I was a little girl from the rural South with a huge dream and no way of making it come true. Or, in my self-pity, that's what I'd come to believe.

Then one day my dad was in the backyard smoking a brisket and reading a book. He was never one to offer an opinion just to hear himself talk. He told me to pull up a chair. "You know, Cathy," he said. "Just because you didn't make it this time doesn't mean you'll never make it. There's nothing to say you can't try again. You haven't lost anything."

I mulled this over for a few days, then I sat down and wrote the people at the Culinary Institute a letter, first apolo-

or could I easily produce the flawless gin-clear consommé r instructors insisted upon, but I was focused and confi- nt.

We were graded hard not just on our cooking but on our pearance. We showed up each morning in full chef regalia— ack shoes, checked pants, white jacket, necktie, and nine- ch toque. People with long hair had to keep it pulled back d neat. I wore a ponytail, but as I worked in the hot kitchen eces of hair slipped out of the elastic. To solve this I went a tle punk, shaved the sides of my head so that when I wore y toque the only visible hair was my ponytail at the back of y head. The sides were shaved clean.

Every morning shoes polished. Necktie just so. Spot- ss whites. Toque balanced on my ponytail. People were pressed. They wondered whether I'd been in the military. he shaved-sides-of-the-head thing became a trend. There re only six women in my class—the most they'd ever admit- d in a single class in the school's history—and all but one aved the sides of their heads.

Until the Culinary, I hadn't given much thought to my sential friendlessness. I had my family and Hannah, but I dn't made any real friends since Wingfield High School. ollege had been fraught with doomed romantic entangle- ents and mostly mind-numbing coursework. I'd steered ear of clubs and organizations where I might actually meet rangers who would become friends.

Now, suddenly, I had a girl gang, a posse of likeminded males, and I was giddy.

My two best friends (just like high school the rule of super- tives didn't apply) were Lorilynn and Kristin. Lorilynn was ll, Julia Child size, with red hair and a big laugh. Kristin was Jersey girl, also big and boisterous. I was more than a foot

gizing for having wasted anyone's time, then explaining that I was so enthusiastic about their program and the possibili- ties it offered that I never considered the culture shock that would befall me. It was difficult for me to admit it, but I told them I had simply been overwhelmed. I told them I wanted to reenroll and give it another shot.

These were the days before email became the preferred method of communication. I waited for the mailman. Finally the letter came. The people at the Culinary Institute were gra- cious in their response, suggesting I take a year to get some more restaurant experience under my belt before returning to Hyde Park to begin again. They ended by saying they were looking forward to having me back.

Then and now, having something to prove lights a fire under me. Since my abuse at the hand of AH, I'd always strug- gled with feelings of worthlessness, and failure tended to stir up that original feeling. Therapy was years in the future, but one day I would understand that for good or for ill, having something to prove motivated me to push hard to succeed, to show to myself and the world that I was a good person capa- ble of excellence.

Shortly afterward, I got a job at the University Club, a private dining club in Jackson. As luck would have it, the executive sous chef had just graduated from the Culinary Institute and knew the ropes. Paul was a Yankee through and through, a short guy with a huge personality and a thick Philly accent. My initial impression was that he was possibly the biggest jerk I'd ever met, but perhaps it was just a matter of getting used to one another, because one day we just started getting along. I confessed that I'd washed out of his alma mater, and wanted to learn anything he had to teach me. Perhaps he viewed me as a diamond in the rough, but Paul made it his mission to get me ready. I became his project.

He drilled me on my knife skills, required me to take the concept of *mise en place* seriously. From the French "putting in place," it means assembling, peeling, grating, cutting, and measuring all your ingredients before you begin to cook. This is the foundation of the chef's ability to turn out perfect dishes quickly and seemingly effortlessly. He taught me how to make a flawless stock and from that a flawless sauce. The standards for soups at the Culinary were legendary: consommé must be so clear you can read the date on a dime at the bottom of the pot.

I knew I knew how to cook, but I'd also developed bad habits. He pointed them out to me and implored me to correct them before I went back north. He taught me how to roast, grill, and sauté with the necessary speed, efficiency, and consistency. On a given evening a home cook might grill a few pork chops; in a restaurant she grills a few dozen, and they all have to be perfect and identical. He taught me how to butcher with confidence. He put me on every station in the kitchen. I prepped, worked the flattop firing meat and fish, made cold appetizers and soups, and prepared desserts. Every trick and technique Paul had in his arsenal he generously passed on to me.

I also accumulated the necessary burns and cuts to teach me how to move with grace and efficiency in a small kitchen. Once, minutes before dinner service, I was cleaning something on the fryer with a long hamburger spatula. I was working away, really leaning into it, when the spatula slipped and slapped the hot oil, sending it splashing down my arm. It was easily a second-degree burn, but someone slapped on some

ointment, wrapped it, and the orders were cor
was on the grill and I kept cooking.

I had a bucket of ice water on the floor b
every five minutes or so I would unwrap my ar
it into the bucket to draw the heat off the bur
that way all night. Grill up a burger or steak, p
my arm into the bucket. Grill it, plate it, plunge
service was over and the kitchen was spotless dic
to the emergency room. That day it became cle
I possessed the proper amount of determinati
and sheer crazy to make it as a chef.

I cut myself every day for months on end.
tips of my fingers and nicked my knuckles. Onc
blade edge of a falling knife with my open hand

I also learned the most important skill of all
my jacket clean. I learned not to wipe my hand
not to put down a pan so hard that it splashe
my sleeve through a hotel pan of marinara
squirt myself with demi-glace, purée, or vinai
lean against a dirty counter that needs to be w
clean jacket for the duration of service tells the v
know what you're doing, and by the time I left
Club and returned to the Culinary Institute of
jacket was spotless. Alongside the skills he pas
Paul taught me to be confident. I've lost track o
years, but I remain grateful for his kindness.

A year later the stars aligned for me at the Culin
mal training at the University Club served me
I breezed through the first month with only a fe
sodes of nerves. I didn't have the world's greate

shorter than Lorilynn (she's six four, I'm five two), and we developed a shtick whereby every day at lunch we'd make an entrance. I stood between her and Kristen, bent my arms at a ninety-degree angle, and they would lift me up by my elbows and carry me in.

In our few spare moments away from the kitchen we liked to shoot pool, and it was during one such game that one of them said, "You're up, Cat."

From that moment on I was Cat Cora. Only my family, close friends, and therapist still call me Cathy.

I also rediscovered my love of extracurriculars. I was vice president of the Epicures of Wine Club, vice president of the Gourmet Society and also coeditor of a self-published student cookbook. We solicited recipes from other students, and created a contest where they had to cook their proposed dishes in order to have their recipes included in the book. We called the book *Kitchen Aid*, and all the proceeds went to charity.

Hannah had decided this time around she would come with me. We rented a beautiful little place in Rhinebeck—a ten-minute drive from campus—a loft apartment with a big picture window overlooking the Hudson. Rhinebeck is a picturesque town, with many historical plaques, antiques shops, and Dutch-style architecture, a holdover from the early settlers. I surprised myself a little by falling in love with it.

I needed a part-time job to pay expenses and help with my student loans, and landed one in the Tavern at the Beekman Arms. The inn bills itself as the oldest continuously operated hotel in the nation. The adjacent restaurant continued the colonial theme, with overhead beams and an open fireplace, and served butternut squash soup, braised short ribs, and Atlantic salmon. The place was owned by renowned chef Larry Forgione, one of the founders of the New American

Cuisine movement, which was exploding across the culinary landscape. My boss was an executive chef named Melissa Kelly. She was my kind of woman, enthusiastic and creative, a cheerful perfectionist. I'd never worked for a woman before, and we got on like a house on fire.

Since Hannah and I returned from Europe and I landed my job at Amerigo, she enjoyed hearing about my culinary antics and became interested in how the front of the house worked. She thought she might like to try her hand at restaurant management one day, and when there was an opening for a waitress at the Beekman, I suggested she apply, and they hired her immediately. You'd be hard-pressed to find a female student who hasn't spent a stint waitressing, and for this reason we tend to think it's a job pretty much anyone can do. Anyone can do it well enough to keep from being fired, but to excel at service you need to be mentally organized, quick on your feet, and unflappable, and Hannah possessed all of these skills. We made enough money to pay the bills and also tour around the Hudson Valley on our few days off. We were happy.

In the summer between your first and second years at the Culinary you're required to do an externship, the idea being that nothing furthers a culinary education more than a few months in a real-world restaurant kitchen. My ambition was on fire after the success of my first year, and I wanted to extern in Manhattan. New York was the culinary capital of the world and no other place would do.

I landed a spot with Anne Rosenzweig, who was all about giving female chefs a shot. She was chef-owner of the celebrated Arcadia, one of the hottest restaurants on the Upper

East Side. She was one of the first to champion so-called American cuisine, which she served with a cheeky twist. I just loved it. Her club sandwich was a lobster club made with roasted vegetables, bacon, and lemon mayonnaise, and was big enough for two people to split. Her Caesar salad was made not with ho-hum romaine, but with then-exotic arugula. She served corn cakes topped with crème fraîche and rack of lamb drizzled with pomegranate juice. What impressed me most was her flair for plating a dish, her feeling for colors, shapes, and textures. Many years later, when I competed on *Iron Chef* and I would smoke the competition with my creative plating skills, I remembered Anne.

Working in her tiny kitchen felt like joining the cast of a movie. I worked under Linda, the daytime sous chef, a hard-ass straight out of some New Jersey industrial town whose accent was so strong I could hardly understand her. The other sous chef was a Moroccan man named Medhi, the hardest worker I'd ever seen. He was a devout Muslim and fasted on the required holidays, working the grill all day long, the sweat pouring off him, but never taking even a sip of water until sundown. I was constantly worried that I'd have to call 911 when he passed out from dehydration, hamburger spatula in hand.

Hannah stayed in Rhinebeck. She wasn't keen on living in Manhattan, and who could blame her? The plan was for me to live in the city during the week and come home on the week-ends. I found a position as a live-in cook for an older couple who worked as journalists. I had my own quarters in a door-man building on Park Avenue. I thought I was set, living the life in New York, New York.

For the first few weeks of my externship my hosts were out of the country, covering some big story somewhere or other, and I had the run of the house. I missed Hannah. I may as well confess it now: I'm a spoiled titty baby. I don't like being away from home, away from my partner, sleeping in a strange bed with the always-weird sheets—why are the sheets of others, no matter the thread count or expense, always unsatisfactory?—and the not-quite-right pillows. Sleeping alone. I didn't like it then and I don't like it now, although I've had to adapt.

But in 1994, I still struggled with being out there alone in the world. I was determined to suck it up. How could I be a bad-ass, world-class chef if I couldn't be away from home? I was like the grown-up version of the third-grader who begs to be picked up from the slumber party because the thought of not sleeping in her own bed is terrifying.

I was able to keep it together until the journalist couple came home. I realize my room and board was predicated on my being their cook, but in less than a week, in addition to having me make breakfast, lunch, dinner, and any number of random snacks, they were also leaving their dirty laundry in a basket in front of my door.

That was it. I quit on the spot and moved back to Rhinebeck, joining the ranks of suburban commuters, taking the train five days a week into the city from Poughkeepsie. I wound up enjoying myself. I had to be at the restaurant at 8:30 a.m., so I had to catch the six o'clock train. I'd grab a coffee and the newspaper, and have that hour and a half to myself to relax and collect my thoughts for the day. Once I arrived I'd hop onto the subway and be at Arcadia in a matter of minutes. At the end of the day, on the way home, I would head back to Grand Central, grab a cold Heineken and the *New York Post,* and sit back to enjoy the quiet time on the train. Even though I thought it was compulsory to do your externship in the city, I found a sweet rhythm in the life of a commuter, and I remember it as a happy time.

⁓

That fall, Nancy, one of the six women in our class at the Culinary, was awarded a "scholarship" to spend a day with Julia Child at her home in Cambridge. Coincidentally, Nancy was Melissa Kelly's aunt, and was a little older than the rest of us, perhaps in her late forties. She was medium height, athletic, and lively, with a thatch of salt-and-pepper hair, maternal in a "you go, girl!" sort of way.

The day with Julia included lunch and the chance to watch her film an episode of her PBS series, *Cooking with Master Chefs*. Julia was always ahead of the curve, and this show, where Julia traveled around the country cooking with top chefs from every region (in the companion cookbook, Julia interpreted the recipes on the show for the home cook), could have sprung from the Food Network brain trust just last week.

Nancy was allowed to bring a guest, and after class one day, as I was putting away my knives, she came up to me, told me about her prize, and said, "I can't think of anyone else who would appreciate an afternoon with Julia more than you."

I practically keeled over with joy. I hugged her so hard she claimed she saw stars.

Chicago chef Rick Bayless was Julia's guest on the show that day. They filmed in Julia's kitchen on Irving Street in Cambridge, with its extra-high counters, the only concession she'd made when she remodeled. Otherwise, it didn't look a whole lot different from my mother's kitchen on Swan Lake Drive, with its double oven and nothing-special refrigerator. Despite her wealth, Julia never wanted anything special—read "professional"—in her kitchen, because she never wanted to alienate her devoted audience of regular home cooks.

I'd never watched anything filmed before. Julia, in her hot pink blouse and purple scarf, was an old pro, asking Rick Bayless pertinent questions and effortlessly leading him on to the next step. Rick had a lot of brown hair and schoolboy glasses. When we sat down to lunch at Julia's kitchen table, covered with a practical wax-coated tablecloth, I suddenly felt shy. She was just as she had been at the book signing—interested, engaged, twinkly eyed—but I was sure she wouldn't remember me. How many thousands of people did she meet in a year?

"I'm sure you don't remember me, but I met you at a book signing in Natchez. Mississippi. I was the girl from Jackson who asked you about becoming a chef. You said go to the CIA, it's the Harvard of cooking schools, and that's what I did. I'm graduating in a few weeks."

"Oh, of course, that's splendid!" said Julia, seeming to mean it.

Did she remember, or was she just being polite? I prefer to think that she'd seen something in me, and it made me feel good knowing I hadn't let her down.

In early 1995 I graduated from the Culinary Institute with honors, at the top of my class. Twelve years later, I would be invited back to give a commencement speech.

⟿ ten ⟿

January 18, 1995

Dear Mademoiselle Cora:
    We regret to inform you that we are unable to offer you a position with us at this time. As has been our policy since our doors opened seventy years ago, we do not allow women into our kitchen. Nevertheless, we wish you the best of luck in your future endeavors.

Sincerely,
Monsieur X

It was the eighth rejection I'd received in as many days. I'd painstakingly composed a letter describing my accomplishments and goals, assembled clippings from the Culinary Institute newspaper highlighting my achievements, collected glowing recommendations from my most exacting instructors, and mailed my application to ten of France's top three-star restaurants.

Every graduate at the Culinary who aspired to be an executive chef in a good restaurant was encouraged to do a *stage* (the French pronunciation has a soft *a* and rhymes with *collage*), an unpaid internship in a French kitchen. The French invented restaurants, and before the advent of the modern cooking school, young aspiring chefs learned their trade through the

95

ancient tradition of apprenticeship. In modern times, it gives a cook the chance to hone his—and most of the time it is a *he*—skills out there in the real fine-dining world, where every dish that leaves the kitchen is expected to be perfect.

My first choice was Paul Bocuse's L'Auberge du Pont de Collonges in Lyon. He turned me down with such speed I doubt he even opened the envelope. I also tried Frédy Girardet, a Swiss chef whose self-named three-star restaurant near Lausanne is one of the best in the world; pretty much everyone who can make a decent roux considers Girardet to be one of the greatest chefs of the twentieth century. He, too, said *non, merci.* No women allowed in his kitchen, either, and no apologies for the blatant sexist attitude. That's just the way it was.

I turned twenty-eight in April of that year and was getting powerfully cranky in the face of all these roadblocks. What if every French chef I'd approached said no? I could apply for internships in Italy, Spain, or Germany, but it wasn't the same. In the mid-nineties, it was France or don't waste your time and money.

Then my luck changed. One day I received two acceptances in the mail—one from Georges Blanc, who owned the restaurant that carried his name, in Vonnas, and the other from Roger Vergé in Mougins. After years of grilling, sautéing, chopping, mincing, grinding; of working, networking, hoping, and dreaming, it was finally happening. I said yes to both, without giving a single thought to how exactly I was going to afford it.

Aside from a single meal a day, my *stages* at Georges Blanc and at Roger Vergé's restaurant, Le Moulin de Mougins, would be on my own dime. Even if I succeeded in deluding myself that I could work hard and live on one meal a day, I'd still have to contend with the matters of lodging, airfare to France, train fare from Vonnas to Moulins, and all the incidentals I would need during the six months I would be abroad. In all my grand dreaming, I had a habit of forgetting about basics like shampoo, toothpaste, money for laundry, and the occasional beer I might want to grab at the end of a long day.

I borrowed a little money from my parents, and my grandmom insisted on pulling some out of her savings. I took extra shifts at work, did some catering on the side. I drew up a budget so tight I already felt dizzy with hunger. Still, I could make it work. Six weeks after I'd received my acceptance letter and two weeks after I graduated from the Culinary, in March 1995, I was on a plane to France.

⟳

I flew to Lyon and was met at the airport by Achille and Stavri, old Greek friends of Taki and Maria, my godparents. They were a modern European couple who lived separately during the week. Achille was quiet, a gynecologist with a practice in the city, and he stayed in their apartment in Lyon. Stavri was a professor and intellectual who preferred the country, and stayed in their beautiful stone farmhouse in the hills of San Belle, a small village not far from Lyon. She was small and feisty, with an easy laugh. They were opposites who enjoyed one another's company, but also had, I'd heard, "arrangements."

I struggled to stay awake as they drove, filling me in on the details of their farmhouse's restoration, the challenges of finding a good stonemason, and the rest I've forgotten, because I may have lost the battle and fallen asleep. The next morning they drove me to the village of Vonnas, an hour north, toward the Swiss border.

We drove through Vonnas proper on our way to my accommodations. Vonnas is Georges Blanc land. In the early nineties he bought the village bakery and grocery store. Then in a move straight out of Monopoly, he purchased seventeen of the ancient houses surrounding his restaurant, creating a *village gourmand* of shops, cafes, and hostelries. The little village was romantic and pristine, the style uniformly Alpine. I was beginning to feel the same stirrings of panic and homesickness I'd experienced during my first stint at the Culinary, but the quaint beauty calmed me. I could live here for three months, couldn't I?

Except I wasn't going to be living in the cozy, charming, well-lit center of Vonnas. Achille continued through the village and up a steep hill into a neighborhood that was as dreary as the *village gourmand* was charming.

My new home was a squat, three-story concrete building that looked like some kind of asylum for the criminally insane. I thought maybe it was just me, jet-lagged, anxious, nervous, but then I saw Achille and Stavri exchange worried looks. Giving me a sidelong glance, Achille saw my face, the downturned corners of my mouth, and leapt out of the car, hustled my suitcase out of the trunk of the Peugeot, and assured me that this place would grow on me in a few weeks' time.

They helped me carry my luggage to the second floor. I wasn't surprised to see that my cell was similar to that found in a white-collar prison (at least according to *Law & Order*). We said our good-byes, and my last connection to home and my old life hopped into their blue Peugeot and drove back down the hill.

After I unpacked my suitcase I decided I would feel better if I had something to eat. The thought cheered me up just a bit. I was here because of my love of food, and food would help me appreciate being here. With a new sense of purpose

I trudged back down the hill to the village in the drizzle. But it was Sunday, and I'd forgotten, if I ever knew, that in most European towns and villages, shops are closed on Sunday. Everything in Vonnas was closed. By the time I'd circled the village in search of something, anything to eat, I was soaked to the bone, my teeth chattering.

My resolve was fragile. I came upon a phone booth. Inside it was warmer and smelled only slightly of BO and urine. I used my calling card to call home. My mom answered on the first ring, as if she'd been expecting me. The sound of her voice reminded me just how far away from home I was.

"I think I may have made a mistake," I cried.

"Don't worry, honey," she said. "You did not make a mistake. You just need to settle in."

"How do you know?" I pleaded.

"Because it's your dream," she said.

As much as I could see myself repacking my suitcase, paying all the money I'd so carefully saved to a taxi driver to take me back to Lyon, where I would buy a ticket for the next flight home to Jackson, I couldn't imagine telling Georges Blanc I was wussing out. However terrible I felt in this moment, I'd come too far. And I felt angry at myself for not being made of sterner stuff.

By the time I hiked back up the hill it was dark. My stomach squawked with hunger, but I put on three layers of clothes to stay warm, then climbed into bed. All night long I heard talking, moaning, and the occasional scream coming from the floor above me. Later I would learn that the top floor served as the village's residential psychiatric treatment facility, a polite way of saying Vonnas's mental institution. Not far from what I'd guessed.

Things did look better in the morning. On my first day in

the kitchen of a world-renowned Michelin three-star restaurant, excitement overrode my nerves. It had been a day since I'd eaten and my head was pounding for lack of coffee. I set off on the twenty-minute walk down the hill, along the slick cobblestone streets that lead to restaurant Georges Blanc, arriving a little before 7:00 a.m.

I'd imagined that cooks would just be arriving, sleepy-eyed and beginning their prep, but the kitchen was in full swing, with pots clanging, cooks issuing orders to the *commis*, the junior chefs, in French. A quick glance around the kitchen confirmed what I'd suspected: that even though Georges Blanc had accepted me, he ran an almost exclusively male kitchen. That morning I saw no women at work, but later I would meet Greta, whose buzz cut and big shoulders gave her a bad-ass military mien, and Kimiko, one of a team of highly trained Japanese chefs there to learn nouvelle cuisine.

The introductions were short and in French. I spoke only what I'd learned at the Culinary. It was alarmingly obvious that I was going to have to get up to speed *tout de suite*. For now, I relied on the international language of cooking—pointing, nodding, and eyebrow waggling. When no one barked or threw anything, I assumed I got it right.

The pastry chef, Marco, who worked directly under Georges Blanc, permitted me to grab a croissant and *café crème* before reporting to the *chef garde manger*, the chef in charge of cold dishes—appetizers, salads, pâtés, terrines.

He assigned me to asparagus peeling. No problem. At the Culinary I'd developed a serious affection for the vegetable and knew I could do the best peeling job in the history of Georges Blanc. I took up my position at a long counter beside a *commis* who seemed no older than twelve. He looked like a child dressed up as a chef for Halloween, in his baggy checked pants, white jacket, and white pleated toque that was half as tall as he was.

Despite the rise of the cooking school, the old apprenticeship system is still alive and well in the great kitchens of France. Many families still send their sons off to be trained before they're old enough to shave. One *commis* at Georges Blanc had already worked in three kitchens by the time he was thirteen.

The twelve-year-old *commis* and I were about the same size. In a small, crowded kitchen with hot stoves, big steaming pots, and knives, being small and compact was an advantage. I picked up an asparagus spear and set to work with a vegetable peeler, depositing the curls of the fibrous outer layer in a tidy pile. The asparagus was going to be used in a black truffle asparagus salad. I felt a weird surge of pride: my peeled asparagus contributing to the one of the world's best restaurant's signature dishes.

Beside me the *commis* was working his way through a big stainless steel bowl of chives. One of the marks of a three-star kitchen is that every step is executed with perfection. His cuts needed to be uniform and precise, but also executed quickly. He was rushing through the job, tossing some of the ends into the trash instead of setting them aside to be made into oil. In any kitchen wasting food is tantamount to stealing money from the register, but at a place like Georges Blanc that kind of shortcut is high treason. It's not just the waste that offends, but also the mediocre technique that leads to it.

The executive chef was an older guy of perhaps fifty, Jean-Claude. He had a face that looked as if it had been lifted straight from an old French painting: beaky nose, small eyes, and crumpled mouth. He was strolling around the kitchen with his arms crossed, overseeing our work. I was focused on

and work, not splurge on local cuisine. And anyway, there would be plenty of fabulous, refined meals in my future that I would have a hand in both creating and savoring, and that thought helped me tough it through can after can of ravioli.

One night, back at the dorm, I was hunched over the stovetop in the common room, and I felt a light tap on my shoulder. It was Kimiko, one of the Japanese chefs. She pointed to the orange globs simmering in the saucepan and shook her head. Then she removed the pot from the burner and gestured to a bag of groceries on the counter. An hour later, I joined her and her countrymen for a delicious meal of stuffed quail, golden tempura, and a cheap but good bottle of white wine.

Once I settled in, I realized I'd landed at Georges Blanc at the perfect time. Nouvelle cuisine, which he'd helped pioneer, was having its moment. It included lighter, fresher interpretations of French food infused with exotic, unexpected ingredients like saffron or vanilla, plated simply. This new style was shaking up the old guard of French cooking. In my darker moments I'd wondered whether there was actually a point to doing a *stage* in France, or whether it was simply another hoop to jump through. But as I got more comfortable, I realized how fortunate I was to be at the beating heart of this new movement, learning from its founder how to create its signature dishes. After I got over the initial culture shock, I began to feel as if I belonged. Mississippi was home, but I'd always felt the deep urge to be out in the world. And now that I was, I wanted nothing more than to excel in Georges Blanc's kitchen, creating exquisite dishes, each one inspired, sublime, and flawless. I'd been hungry for that level of commitment, perfection, and engagement my whole life. My contributions were important and appreciated. Ultimately, my gender made no difference. My sexual orientation made no difference. My

height made no difference, nor did my funny accent.
cook. That was all that mattered.

Six weeks into my *stage* I found my groove. I
through each station. I cleaned fifty pounds of pota
one go. I peeled and chopped pounds of vegetables ha
in the morning from the kitchen gardens. I helped He
boucher, debone animal carcasses. I assisted Luc, an i
tionally celebrated *pâtissier*, in pouring sugar and asse
his ingredients. I spent five hours picking herbs. I sc
mountains of pots, platters, and utensils at the *plong*
tion until my hands were raw.

Eventually I got out a little and realized that the er
lage was dedicated to gourmet gastronomy. Fine din
the town's heartbeat, and every business, every citizer
to keep it alive and well. Everything that could not b
right outside the restaurant was purchased from the
farmers—enormous morels, exquisite porcini, delecta
fles. Day in, day out I saw ingredients come straight or
ground into the kitchen and out into the dining ro
matter of hours. I had never felt so connected to food

Meat didn't magically appear, cleaned and butche
ready to be cooked. A farmer would deliver the day's
the region's famous blue-footed chicken—*poulet de*
and within twenty minutes the birds would be slau
gutted, and dressed. The chefs wanted to be in charg
entire process, down to burning off the feathers. The v
time-consuming, but resulted in meat that was unma
its tenderness. And, as with everything else at Georg
it exemplified care and excellence.

In the mornings I jumped out of bed, climbed
chef whites, and hoofed it down the hill in the morr
to report to the kitchen by 7:00 a.m. A chorus of *bor*

ça va? greeted the staff as we filed in and fueled up for the long day with croissants and coffee. Then I reported to the station I'd been assigned to and worked like a madwoman until noon.

The family meals served at Georges Blanc were like nothing I'd ever experienced. Braised endive with lamb, lobsters in champagne sauce, composed salads that were works of art. The meals were transcendent, a gift from the chef-owners to the people they relied upon, reminding us daily that we weren't just cooks, we were part of a large, devoted family that worked together to create something beautiful and nourishing to give to others. The way chefs approach the family meal conveys a lot about them. Do they put thought into what to serve? Do they make an effort to make it special? A good chef will use the family meal to bring his staff together and create a sense of camaraderie. It's one of the secrets to running a first-class restaurant, and the family meals at Georges Blanc were beyond compare.

After family meal, we geared up for the dinner shift. My job was simple, yet demanding. Anything the chefs on the line needed, I ran for it. Saucepans, plates, more garnish. I ran with the urgency of an EMT. The energy in the kitchen was both intense and frenetic.

In the dining room the mood was relaxed and tranquil. The chic nineteenth-century decor boasted Louis XIII chairs, floral tapestries on the wall. A roaring fireplace cast the scene in a golden glow. We served a hundred covers a night, dishes such as *poulet de bresse* in foie gras and champagne sauce, *crêpe vonnassienne* with salmon and caviar, pear tart with almond cream and macarons that rivaled those at Ladureé. Georges spent ample time in the front of the house, effortlessly charming his guests, greeting each table between trips to the kitchen, ensuring that the nightly performance was seamless.

There was nothing rock-and-roll about Georges. He was handsome in a quiet way, and looked less like a world-class chef than a country doctor who made house calls. His presence was subdued and commanding. During my three months in his kitchen I would only see him lose his temper once. An American diner had sent a steak back with the complaint that he'd asked for it well done. Georges marched into the kitchen, his mouth set in a line. He tossed the plate onto the counter and yelled, "*Oh merde. Casse-toi.*" Loosely translated in this context as, "Oh shit, fuck off, Americans." All eyes turned to me, as if I was personally responsible for my countryman's poor taste.

"Hey, don't look at me," I said. "I like mine medium rare."

Even though I had cooked under other chefs before I landed at Georges Blanc, I was inspired by Georges's dignity and quiet correctness. I never once saw him in anything other than a spotless, freshly starched white chef's jacket. He was an artist who took pride in every aspect of his profession. That was the kind of chef I wanted to be, and to this day I will never enter a kitchen without a perfectly laundered jacket.

We worked every night until 11:00 p.m. Feet aching, knees aching, hands raw from washing dishes, we would trudge back up to our dorm, climb onto the roof with a bottle of wine, and talk about our favorite chefs and their innovations. Our French was improving rapidly, and we'd sit under the stars and talk about Marco Pierre White's new cookbook or whether anything was truly going on out in California, dreaming about what it would be like to get to that place. Life was good on that rooftop.

By the third month, I was cruising through my sixteen-hour days. The sous chefs, whose respect we'd earned by refusing to quit, or give anything less than 110 percent, would show their appreciation by taking us on tours of nearby villages. Money was tight and I couldn't afford even an extra *café crème* in a cheap cafe, but they insisted on picking up the tab. We indulged in every local fine wine, cheese, and four-course lunch within a hundred miles of Vonnas. We laughed and called it research.

One Monday morning I was summoned by Jean-Claude. "Today you are on the line," he said, without elaborating. I knew my skills were improving, my palate evolving, but clearly Jean-Claude, and perhaps even Georges himself, could see it, too. This was a major promotion, and a serious honor for a mere apprentice. No longer would I be peeling asparagus and fetching saucepans but working with sauces, a notoriously technical and difficult aspect of French cooking. I was practically levitating with confidence: *I'm nailing this! I'm going to be a chef! I am unstoppable!*

Then late one afternoon I was making my way through a "deep six" pan of shallots, one of those enormous professional vessels in which you could easily bathe a toddler. It was brimming with shallots, those Ping-Pong-ball-size bulbs that look like an elongated onion, but have a milder, smoother flavor. I was tasked with peeling and chopping them all, a surefire recipe for carpal tunnel syndrome. After two hours I was about three-quarters of the way through. I grabbed a shallot and beneath it I could glimpse a wink of stainless steel, the bottom of the pan. The end was in sight.

Suddenly, while I was turned toward the pan, I glimpsed my supervising chef coming up on my other side. In one swift motion he swept my pile of chopped shallots into the garbage. "You are not doing this right!" he snapped.

What in the hell was he talking about? I could chop shallots in my sleep. Chopping shallots was one of the first things

I'd mastered back when I learned how to make Taki's Lyon-naise dressing. Furthermore, I had been chopping shallots this way for going on three months and no one had ever said a word. Before I could stop to think about what I was doing, I stormed past him, hurling a "fuck you" before stomping out of the kitchen. I stood outside, my eyes hot with tears. But I was pissed. I wasn't sorry.

He followed me outside. I glared at him, and he stared down at me. I was not about to break eye contact first.

"Cat, do not cry," he finally said. "Get back in the kitchen." His voice was surprisingly calm given an apprentice had just committed the ultimate breach of protocol.

"I'm done. I'm just completely done," I said. I blotted my tears with the heels of my hands, then threw my arms up for good measure, to demonstrate just how done I was.

"You cannot be done. You have come this far. That"—he gestured toward the kitchen door—"that was nothing. Do not let shallots ruin you."

I took a few deep breaths. He was right, of course. Chefs have committed suicide over losing a Michelin star, and on the grand scale of life in a three-star kitchen, this was a minor episode. Nothing less than perfection was acceptable, and my shallots, which I'd chopped a little unevenly, had not been perfect. That was all.

I remembered an incident at the Culinary. One of my instructors threw a pan of salmon filets across the room because they were slightly overcooked. He then bent over and cussed me out, screaming profanities an inch from my nose, like a demented sergeant in an army movie. "Yes, Chef," I'd said. "You're right, Chef." My basic instinct when faced with criticism was to become more determined, not retreat. So what was I doing outside in the weak late-spring sun, with three weeks left to go at Georges Blanc, pitching a fit? That wasn't me. I marched back in the kitchen, filled another "deep six" with shallots, and began again.

⁓

On the last day at Georges Blanc the staff threw me a going-away party. Jean-Claude, Marco, Luc, and the other chefs joked that the party wasn't simply a formality, that there was true cause to celebrate because they hadn't thought I would survive my first week.

Kimiko and my Japanese friends saw me off at the train station. Tokashi, a lanky chef from one of Tokyo's up-and-coming restaurants, insisted on helping me with my bags. He was so concerned that my luggage made it aboard and was properly stowed that the train departed before he'd had a chance to hop off. He just laughed and sat beside me until the next stop, a good hour away.

After we said our final good-byes, I settled back in my seat and gazed out the window. The train headed south, past tidy farms and the famous lavender fields of Provence. I'd survived. I was a different person from the one sniveling into the phone to my mom on that dank Sunday in March, and ten times the chef I'd been before.

~ eleven ~

My arrival in Mougins, a tiny, tree-lined village overlooking the French Riviera, could not have been more different from my arrival in Vonnas. The south of France was sunny and warm, the air infused with lavender, rose, and jasmine from the surrounding fields. Golden. That word kept coming to mind. I was golden as well. In my heart of hearts I knew I would have the life of a chef.

Roger Vergé was an institution in Mougins. He opened Le Moulin de Mougins in 1969, and by 1974 it had already been awarded its third Michelin star. Alain Ducasse, who would go on to become one of the world's most successful and celebrated chefs, the first to own three restaurants in three different cities with three Michelin stars, apprenticed to Vergé, who trained Ducasse in the Provençal style of cooking for which he would become famous. Like Georges Blanc, Roger Vergé was one of the fathers of nouvelle cuisine; part of their mission to modernize French cooking included inviting women to work in their kitchens.

Mougins is perched on a hill above the Mediterranean, fifteen minutes from Cannes, an ancient fortified village with narrow winding streets lined with stone houses. We're talking pre-Roman. From the eleventh century to the French Revolution it was administered by monks. Pablo Picasso spent the

111

last twelve years of his life in a farmhouse down the road from the Moulin, which means mill in French, and Vergé's restaurant was housed in a sixteenth-century olive mill, surrounded by ancient trees.

I went straight from the train station to the restaurant, where I was greeted by Serge, Le Moulin's executive chef. Serge was wiry and bright-eyed, with the energy of a terrier. Immediately, he took me aside. "I must tell you something very important that will affect your time here," he said.

I braced myself. Perhaps my apprenticeship had been canceled? Or, alternatively, a sous chef had quit that morning and I was going to be tossed onto the line, where I would be sure to make a complete fool of myself?

He eyed me carefully to gauge whether I could handle the gravity of his news.

"There are two women who are also doing apprenticeships. But their situation is a little different," he continued. "They paid quite a bit to be here for this opportunity to learn Roger's way of cooking. So, of course, they will be treated to his way of living."

I nodded like a bobblehead, even though I had no idea what he was getting at.

"What this means is you will be treated the same. With long lunches and wine tastings during your evenings off. It is imperative, however, that you don't let on that you are here for free."

"*De rien*," I said. No problem. I guessed at the intrigue. Roger Vergé was running a mini–cooking school course on the side, and didn't want his students to realize that he also offered the traditional *stage* experience, where the apprentice doesn't have to pay for the experience of working in a three-star kitchen. My feelings were mixed. On the one hand, I could use a little break. On the other, I found I'd developed a taste for the adrenaline-fueled rush of service. I was here to work, not sit back and sip rosé and savor the cheese course.

My experience with Georges Blanc had been focused, intense, and businesslike. The goal was always perfection, achieved at any cost. If a dish went out and it wasn't perfect by the standards set in the kitchen, it was a failure, even if the guest found it delicious and would go on to rave about it for the rest of his life.

Roger was just as serious about producing a three-star experience, but his approach was laid-back. He took the French concept of joie de vivre and applied it to cooking. He thought the whole experience, from sourcing the ingredients to sitting with his guests enjoying an after-dinner aperitif, should be joyous. Understandable, given the weather, the sun-drenched hills covered with olive trees, the acres of lavender and *rose de mai*, the faithful sea breeze. Everyone in the Le Moulins kitchen moved through their tasks with a loose-limbed ease, and I never saw anyone treated in a manner that could get you three to five in county jail back in the States. Life was easy in Mougins, even with sixteen-hour days.

Vergé's variety of Provençal cuisine was called *cuisine du soleil*, cuisine of the sun, and had more in common with Mediterranean fare than with classical French cuisine. The local ingredients he favored were familiar from the Greek dishes of my girlhood: eggplant, zucchini, lentils, and of course, olives.

Early one morning, not long after I arrived, I was sent out back to pick garnishes. The day would wind up hot and sunny, but the morning air was chilly and smelled of ocean brine. The sun was cresting over the hill, and I shielded my eyes with my hand, surveying a full acre dedicated to growing edible flowers: delicate purple chive blossoms, soft blue bor-age, lemon verbena. I placed the tiny flowers in a basket on my hip, like a peasant woman of yore. The flowers were hardly an integral part of the meal, but their gorgeous presence on the plate would ensure that a meal was unforgettable.

As at Georges Blanc, our family meals at Le Moulins were first-rate. The bulk of our workday lay ahead of us—we still had to prep for dinner service—but we enjoyed the meal as if we had nothing but time. Serge was a talker. He possessed an encyclopedic knowledge of the local produce, and was a master at preparing it so that the freshness and flavors spoke for themselves. He loved to lecture us on how to hunt for wild mushrooms or grow giant squash blossoms.

One of Le Moulin's signature dishes was constructed around the billowy golden blossoms we grew in the greenhouse. They were ten times the size of any squash blossom I'd seen in my life, and brought to mind bad jokes about plants cultivated in the field next to a nuclear power plant. The dish they starred in was pure decadence. The bottom of each blossom was filled with *duxelles*, a mixture of wild mushrooms, shallots, onions, herbs, and high-quality French butter cooked down into a paste. A golf ball–sized truffle was then pressed into the duxelles, and the mixture was held in place by ends of the petals, which were gathered together and tied off with chives. It was served with a foie gras truffle sauce. And it was only an appetizer.

On my days off I'd take the local bus down the hill to Cannes. I'd walk for an hour or so, then stop for lunch in an outdoor cafe, where I'd treat myself to a plate of fresh mussels and write letters home, one to my parents and Grandmom, one to Hannah.

Drowsy and buzzed from the wine, I'd wander down to the beach, where I joined the topless locals, lying on my back in the sand, worshipping the sun. I felt young, free, and adventurous.

One day after this ritual, I went to the bank of phone booths I usually used to call home. I called Hannah, and while we talked, an exquisite French girl came into the next booth. She stared at me as she carried on her own conversation. After she completed her call and disappeared into the crowd, I kicked myself for not speaking to her.

I'd been in France for nearly six months by this time, and even though Hannah had been supportive of my taking the apprenticeships, she'd grown restless and fed up with waiting for me to come home. She complained often that she felt like her life was on hold, waiting in our Rhinebeck apartment, staring out the big picture window at the Hudson.

During a recent phone call she'd said, "It's always all about *you*, Cathy." I couldn't argue with her. I knew it had been a lot to ask. But on the other hand, she'd never claimed to be anything but 100 percent behind my ideas and schemes, happily quitting her job at Allstate to backpack through Europe, throwing herself into creating the business plan for our ill-fated Caribbean concept restaurant, enduring our separation during my first unsuccessful stint at the Culinary, pulling up stakes and moving north with me to Rhinebeck for my second successful go-round, and now waiting while I completed my *stages* in France. We were at an impasse. Before I'd arrived in Mougins, during yet another tense phone call, we decided to take a break from our relationship. We kept up with our weekly calls and we still cared about one another deeply, but our relationship was on hold.

Wandering around Cannes on that summer afternoon, occasionally stopping in at a shop just to feel the pleasure of using my now nearly fluent French, I considered my future. My experience in France had given me everything I would need to be a chef—confidence, courage, and the best training in the world. I had no job waiting for me at home, and with the experience I'd gained with Georges and Roger, I could easily find a job in any kitchen in Europe. I tried to imagine myself in a small French village, or even Paris, arriving at work in the blue dawn, returning home to an empty flat on a cobblestoned street. I couldn't make the image stick. My goal, I realized then, was to make it as a chef in America.

~ twelve ~

Sometime between our last, frustrating weekly call and wheels down on the tarmac in New York, Hannah had met someone else. She confessed that they'd kissed, and the rest I didn't want to think about.

During the first month I was home, in the midst of my jet lag and growing freak-out that I had no job and no prospects, I tried to woo her. I cooked for her, took her out to the movies, and listened for what seemed like hours on end to what it was like for her to be the one left behind. While we'd been together she'd been so sweet and accepting, just happy, it seemed, to be in a loving relationship. I'd been a jackass, self-absorbed, with jobs, work, school, ambition, travel, my apprenticeships. So self-absorbed that I hadn't noticed her growing and changing. Now she wouldn't warm up to me, had no interest. She was indifferent verging on coldhearted. I remembered suddenly how impressed I'd been when we first met, that she'd been out and proud despite the disapproval of pretty much everyone she knew. I was reminded she had a backbone.

I deserved exactly what I got. During our years together I *had* taken her for granted. I'd had my own flirtations and make-out sessions with other girls. At the Culinary I'd been with two sexy straight women, one a school executive. Both had made it clear they were interested in experimenting and thought I would be a good gateway girl into the lesbian world. Once, when Hannah and I were in a rocky patch, I had a fling with a gorgeous blonde with a Hawaiian name. Maluhia was one of the most beautiful women I'd ever laid eyes on. We both felt the electricity the day we traded glances in the crowded halls of the Culinary. We had a few encounters, our passion torrid but short-lived. Eventually it became clear that she loved men more, and I knew I loved my relationship more.

One night soon after I arrived home from France, I cooked *kota kapama* for Hannah, the first time I'd made it since I'd been home. Our apartment was filled with the scent of garlic and cinnamon, smells I equated with comfort and love. Hannah came home from work, took one look at what was on the stove, and made a face. Only then did it occur to me that she had truly moved on.

My months in France, exhilarating as they'd been, had left me wrung out, flat broke, and in no mood to be spurned on a daily basis. A picture of us in a frame sat on the bedside table. The next day while she was at work I slipped the picture out of the frame, packed the suitcase and duffel bag it felt like I'd just unpacked, scratched a little note on the back of an envelope, and drove home to Mississippi.

I'd called my parents, told them I was headed down for a visit and some southern-style TLC. I pulled into the driveway and not one thing had changed on Swan Lake Drive. The huge pines in front of the house were still shedding needles. The pool table in the sunroom was covered with the same stacks of papers I'd glimpsed the last time I'd been home. I had been away long enough, and was still young enough, to note that my parents had aged a bit in my absence. They were as sharp and warm as always, but their movements were a little stiffer, their hair a smidge grayer. Alma, who'd been old as long as I'd been alive, was in the kitchen making a cheesecake in anticipation of my homecoming.

I'd just missed my brother Mike, who against all odds had landed on his feet. After he was released from the county farm, the judge had advised him that since he owed so many people money it was probably best if he moseyed down the road to another state. For a while he laid low on Flag Island, the site of our happiest summers, living off the fish he caught and figuring out his next move. He disappeared for a while then showed up in Little Rock, where he worked for the owner of a gas station and then at a hauling business. Finally he started a wrecking business with some friends and snagged contracts with the fire and police department, hauling away cars that had been totaled in accidents. He'd had a short-lived marriage, but then met a stand-up citizen named Carrie, who by all reports was good for him.

I moved back into my old bedroom on Swan Lake Drive, my softball trophies from grammar school still lined up on the dresser. Four, five, six days passed with no call from Hannah. The days were mercifully mild after the brain-boiling heat of summer, which I was not unhappy to have missed. Driving past my old high school, I sometimes heard the marching band practicing. It was football season in the South. Fall was in the air.

I'm the first to admit that between graduating at the top of my class at the Culinary and not simply surviving but thriving in two French three-star kitchens, I'd become a little snooty. The first day I joined my mom in the kitchen I picked up one of her knives and touched my thumb to the blade.

"You need some new knives, Mom."

"Says who?"

"Just about every great chef out there," I said.

"Cathy, you know, just because you graduated from cooking school and spent a few months among the French, don't you come in here trying to tell me how to cook."

She took the knife out of my hand and pointed it at me. She was joking, but she also meant it. She was opposed to me or anyone getting too comfortable up on her high horse. She believed that if you've done great things, that's for someone else to say.

Down the road the values my mom and dad instilled in me would surface in the way I treated my own brigades and eventual business partners. I would surround myself with people who were smart, creative, and productive, who would work hard and tell me the truth. I wouldn't hire people who told me what they thought I might like to hear.

After a week, Hannah phoned late one night. She said all the things that lure a person back into love. She missed me, hadn't realized how much she loved me until I was gone, couldn't bear the thought of life without me. She'd dumped the girl she'd been hooking up with. I spent a few more weeks at home, then returned to Rhinebeck, and we settled right in as if nothing had happened, both of our transgressions forgotten.

I'm a firm believer that things happen for a reason, and not a day after I'd returned to New York I received a call from Melissa Kelly, my old executive chef from the Beekman Arms.

"I heard you're back from France," she began in the abrupt, get-right-to-it manner I associate with northerners. "I have this great situation up in Old Chatham. It's a five-hundred-acre sheep farm. The new owners came into a lot of money and want to open an inn and a restaurant. We'll have homegrown ingredients, make our own bread and cheese. You interested?"

"Sure am," I said.

Melissa had also graduated at the top of her class at the Culinary in 1988, and since then had been all over the place, working with Larry Forgione at An American Place in New York, Reed Hearon at Restaurant Lulu in San Francisco, and queen Alice Waters at Chez Panisse. She worked as a private cook in the south of France for a while, and moved to Japan to open another An American Place there. *Food & Wine* had named her one of the best upcoming chefs of the nineties. I'd kept up with her exploits through her aunt, my friend Nancy, the one who invited me to Julia Child's house for lunch.

I guessed that Nancy had told Melissa a little about my exploits as well. In the mid-nineties, even if you were a graduate of the Culinary Institute of America, it remained a big damn deal to get a *stage* in a French kitchen, especially if you were female.

Hannah and I drove to Old Chatham, an hour and a half north up the Hudson River Valley. The farm sat amid rolling hills and was picture-postcard beautiful, with well-kept outbuildings painted traditional barn red with white trim, surrounded by green fields in which a few flocks of sheep in their woolly coats ambled and dozed. Melissa was just as I'd remembered her from the Beekman Arms: pretty, dark-haired, and pale-eyed. She had the thin, strong limbs I associated with farm women or avid hikers. She rubbed her hands as she showed us around, told us how the owners, Tom and Nancy Clark, were going to grow the flock (eventually they would have around two thousand head) and how we were going to have fresh sheep milk to make cheese, ice cream, and crème brûlée. She was already imagining the flavors she would offer, classic vanilla and chocolate, and also rum raisin.

The farm-to-table movement was in its infancy then. Not

everyone who peeled a carrot or washed a lettuce leaf believed that the flavor of a dish depended on where a vegetable was grown and when it was picked. But Melissa had been mentored by Larry Forgione, who along with Alice Waters was leading the farm-to-table parade, and she was well acquainted with what grew in the Hudson Valley from her time at the Beekman Arms.

Twenty years ago it was relatively insane to open a restaurant on a farm in a tiny historic hamlet, located in the middle of a tangle of sleepy country roads, close to absolutely nothing. This wasn't France, where cuisine was the national religion, height of culture, and favorite sport all rolled into one. People who could afford it thought nothing of traveling hundreds of miles to dine at Georges Blanc, including rich Parisians who flew in for the evening in a private helicopter, landing on the helipad installed on the roof especially for such patrons.

We opened the Old Chatham Sheepherding Company Inn together, and from the first we were packed every night. People would come from Albany and Sarasota Springs, even making the two-and-a-half-hour drive from Manhattan. *Esquire* magazine dubbed it one of the top ten restaurants in the country.

One of the main farm-to-table tenets was to follow the ingredients. Freshness and availability determined the menu, not the other way around. For this reason, the menu changed daily. At many restaurants, you show up in your whites at 7:00 a.m., half asleep and clutching a cup of coffee, and shuffle through prep for the institutional chicken dish, pasta dish, and whatever red meat had been on the menu for years. Not the case at the Sheepherding Co. For a long time, it was as if every day was my first day on the job.

Lamb was on the menu a lot, obviously: rack of lamb served on a bed of broccoli rabe and garlic mashed potatoes;

char-grilled lamb served with beet greens and huckleberries, with a side of sweet potato chips; lamb shanks, leg of lamb, and lamb shoulder chop.

Melissa was Italian on her mother's side, and we shared a similar grounding in Mediterranean cuisine. We served sheep's cheese in grape leaves with thyme, rosemary, savory, lavender, and cracked black pepper, marinated overnight in olive oil, then grilled and served with flatbread. Eggplant caponata, with capers and anchovies, finished with a thick sweet-and-sour sauce of brown sugar, vinegar, and tomato puree. A simple, delicious panna cotta, and of course sheep's milk ice cream, which was sweet and rich and had a slight tang I can still taste.

That daily menu change kept me on my toes, expanded what I'd mistakenly thought of as my already extensive repertoire. I incorporated quinoa and farro into my kitchen vocabulary. I learned a few dozen ways to use fresh figs, Meyer lemons, and the new heirloom tomatoes that were just coming on the scene. I could make a hundred sauces in my sleep.

The Sheepherding Co. started showing up on best-of lists and in feature spreads in newspapers, and was winning awards. Every week, it seemed, a van arrived from Manhattan, and out poured photographers and writers, there to cover Melissa and her amazing, unexpected success. I may have been racing around making sure service happened that night, but I saw what was going on. I saw what she'd earned, and I wanted a chance to do that for myself.

The inn and restaurant were housed in an eighteenth-century Georgian colonial manor, and the kitchen was as tiny as any you'd find in Manhattan. For a solid year Melissa and I worked shoulder to shoulder, like two oxen yoked together, plowing the fields. After I started feeling the stirrings of ambition, however, things changed. Melissa, like any good executive chef, commanded her kitchen like an army general. *Sous* means under in French, and they don't call it sous chef for nothing. I was eager to be the one creating the menu and plate design, evolving the concept of the restaurant, and in general not having to take orders from anyone else. I wanted to be the one who came up with an idea for a new dish at midnight, called for a quick meeting of my staff, and saw customers order and enjoy it the next night. I wanted to be in charge. And I'm not afraid to admit it: I wanted the fame. I wanted to be a star.

Hannah and I, and our two Greyhound rescue dogs, barely survived the historic blizzard of 1996, months after we arrived in Old Chatham. We'd never witnessed such a thing, fifty-mile-an-hour wind gusts, barns and grocery store roofs collapsing under the weight of many feet of snow, people stranded in buses for hours and days, the government shuttered for a week. A year later, on the first day the temperature dipped below zero, we looked at each other over our morning coffee and agreed: this is completely insane. We could see our breath in the bathroom of our little rental house, and the dogs shivered in their sleep, even on top of the heat vent. Every day I looked forward to the infernal heat of the kitchen, something that as a Mississippi girl born and raised I could tolerate with relative ease.

Then, sometime in early 1997, the offer I'd been waiting for finally landed. Restaurants fail in record numbers every year. In the time it's taken you to read this chapter, I'm sure another one has shut its doors forever. The Sheepherding Co. was exceptional. All the national coverage had the culinary world buzzing, and somewhere in the buzz, my name had come to the attention of Donna and Giovanni Scala, owners of Bistro Don Giovanni in California's Napa Valley.

Donna Scala called and offered me the position of *chef de cuisine*, or executive chef. I weighed their offer for a good ninety seconds before saying hell yes.

Melissa Kelly's fame and general bad-assery would continue. In 1999 she would win a James Beard Foundation Award for Best Chef in the Northeast, a huge honor, since her competition included the powerhouse chefs of every three-star restaurant in New York. A few months later, in August of that same year, both Melissa and her pastry chef, Price Kushner, would resign from the Sheepherding Co. in order to open Primo, in Rockland, Maine. Even though Melissa claimed she was replaceable, the Clarks, perhaps feeling stressed from the pressure, both financial and personal, of running a nationally renowned inn and restaurant, closed their doors.

~ thirteen ~

had never been west of east Texas, and when Hannah and I arrived in California that spring we were stupid with joy. It was green and balmy, with sunny days and crisp, starry nights. I was reminded of Mougins, that same soft air tinged with lavender, that lemony light. The vibe in Napa was vastly different from any place I'd ever known. Everything grew so easily there. For the first few months, whenever I'd see oranges or lemons hanging from a tree, my first thought was they must be fake. And however cool and happening Melissa's farm-to-table vision had been at Old Chatham, California in the mid-nineties was on the leading edge of American cuisine. The French Laundry, which Ruth Reichl had just called "the most exciting restaurant in America," Thomas Keller's homage to the three-star country restaurants of France, with a California spin, was just down the road. A mere thirty-eight miles to the south, in Berkeley, Queen Alice held court at Chez Panisse, acknowledged by many as the birthplace of California cuisine.

I connected immediately with my new boss, Donna Scala. She was a southern girl, from Virginia, and had also *staged* in some famous kitchens in the south of France. In the early eighties she opened an Italian and French gourmet specialty shop in Sausalito, and then with her husband, Giovanni, opened Piatti Ristorante in Yountville.

Don Giovanni had been open for four years when I came on board. The restaurant was charming and funky, with French doors, terra-cotta tiles, and a lush forest of potted plants that grew without much care that I could see. You could sit out-doors beneath sturdy pergolas shaded by wisteria and strung with tiny white lights. Donna was a madwoman on the sub-ject of decorating, and closed the place down for a month every other year to paint and replace the chairs. She was crazy on the subject of her chairs.

Donna was warm and maternal, and I was immediately attracted to her dark Mediterranean looks. She wasn't very tall, slim when we first met, and hardly looked forty. I was impressed with her pearls, which she wore with her chef's jacket.

I learned a lot from Donna, including how to make a first-class ciabatta and the proper way to caramelize Brussels sprouts. She impressed upon me more than anyone the power and necessity of tasting your food constantly. The concept wasn't new to me, obviously. All along the way, in classes at the Culinary, at my internships in France, and at Old Chatham, I watched while chefs tasted their food. But it had looked more like a habit than the best weapon in your arsenal; Donna taught me otherwise.

I was excited to the point of insomnia about the chance to make my mark. The first thing I noticed upon my arrival was the big laminated ten-page menu. For a second I thought I was back at The Continental in Jackson. That simply wouldn't do. We were closing in on the end of the century. After the Sheepherding Co., who knew better than me the power and appeal of the single-page menu? How easy it would be to draw up a new one each day in Napa, where the local farmers cruised by every morning and allowed me to choose produce straight off the back of their trucks. Heirloom peppers, beautiful emerald-green kale, butter lettuce the size of your head. Valencia oranges and beautiful yellow-fleshed Sugar Time peaches. Anything I could imagine pretty much presented itself most mornings.

I convinced Donna and Giovanni to get rid of the tome, institute a one-page menu, and lose some of the heavier pastas. I suggested we feature more traditional Mediterranean fare, including whole fish (which, I'm proud to say and if memory serves, we were the first to do in the valley), food not unlike what I grew up on, minus the grits and tamales.

One morning on my way to work I noticed the driveway was littered with olives. When I walked back down that night at the end of dinner service, in the moonlight I looked down and saw beautiful plump olives that had been crushed to a pulp beneath the tires of the BMWs and Mercedes driven by our customers. I'd had one of a cook's hard golden rules— never waste a thing—seared into my brain that first day at Georges Blanc. Standing in the driveway, staring down at all those crushed olives, I saw precious olive oil going to waste. It wasn't as if I imagined Bistro Don Giovanni going into the olive oil production business (although, as it would turn out, they would end up bottling enough to sell at the restaurant). I just thought it would be a nice draw to use oil from our own olives in our dishes. We weren't going to get a huge amount of oil from these trees, but we could create an olive oil that was ours alone. Donna's first response was negative. She thought it would be too much work, but over time I convinced her, and that fall, during olive harvest season, with the help of a guy named Jean-Pierre, a friend of a friend who knew about such things, I harvested Don Giovanni's olives and drove them to Frantoio, an Italian restaurant in Mill Valley, at the time the only place in the country with a state-of-the-art olive oil production facility. They made their own olive oil, and also made their press available to other olive growers.

Jean-Pierre and I hit it off immediately. He was very tall for a Frenchman, maybe six four, and had that swashbuckling look—shaved head, goatee, and an earring. We were friends, but occasionally a man comes along about whom I think, *I don't like men, but if I did, I could certainly like you.* We bonded over my olive oil scheme, creating a delicious thick, nutty extra virgin that elevated all of our dishes and drew raves from our customers.

Word got around that Bistro Don Giovanni had a new executive chef who was shaking things up, introducing a new style of fresh, light Mediterranean cuisine, and we began to attract some luminaries. Lovely Barbara Tropp, of China Moon Cafe fame in San Francisco, came in one day and asked to see me after her meal. She said she loved the food, and put her hand on my shoulder. "You're taking care of yourself, right? Making sure your life is balanced?" I smiled and thanked her for her kind concern, even though we both knew "balance" and "executive chef" are two mutually exclusive terms.

Robert Mondavi and his wife were big customers. Napa Valley wines are world famous, and they have Robert to thank. He built the first winery in Napa back in the sixties and turned the entire industry on its ear, categorizing a wine by variety of grape rather than purpose (Pinot Noir rather than red table wine). He was warm and a big hugger. He would always come back into the kitchen and say, "Cat, Cat, what's the whole fish tonight?"

One afternoon as we were prepping for dinner service, Robert walked in the front door with one of my heroes, Jacques Pépin. He explained that Jacques was in town on a book tour and he wanted to try out the new chef in town, the girl cooking over at Bistro Don Giovanni. Donna had already gone home for the day and I was alone in the back of the house and my nerves started tingling, my mind started racing. What on earth does someone cook for Jacques Pépin? *Just do what you do best,* I told myself. You do the whole fish. You do some beautiful sides. You don't need to be anyone but yourself. I put my head down, felt the peace descend, and got to work.

Jacques loved it, squeezed my hand, and told me it was the best meal he'd had on the road. Part of me supposed he could have said that to all the chefs, but I believed he was genuine. His sincerity was confirmed when two weeks later I received a copy of a letter he'd sent to the James Beard Foundation, saying that while on tour he'd eaten at many top restaurants throughout the Bay Area, but the best meal he'd had was mine at Bistro Don Giovanni, and that they should invite me to do a dinner at the James Beard House.

There were downsides working for Donna. Up and down the Napa Valley, she was legendary for her fiery temper. She may have been the owner-chef of Giovanni's, but by hiring me she was giving up control of the kitchen so that she could focus on running the business. She found herself in a common restaurant world predicament: she hired an executive chef because she saw she couldn't do it all, but came to feel— once I'd relieved her of the responsibility of expediting every night and the eyeball-popping, migraine-inducing pressure of getting out the food had been relieved—that perhaps she actually *could* do it all, and what was I doing, taking up space, asserting myself, and collecting a paycheck for the privilege.

Every executive chef worth his salt learns early to handle orders. I was accustomed to chefs screaming in my face, so close I'd be blurry-eyed from their spittle. I could "Yes, Chef!" with the best of them. I did not complain. It was part of my training, and the inner warrior I'd forged at the Culinary and in France allowed me not to take things personally and to pay attention to the work.

But Donna's orders came with a pinch of salt in the wound, meant to make me feel as if I was neither a good cook nor a good leader. When I didn't season the mashed potatoes to her liking and she roared that I didn't have the commitment to be a first-rate chef, I took it hard. I'd come to the job confident and full of spirit, and I was quickly losing both.

Once, on one of my rare days off, my phone rang at the crack of dawn, waking me from a deep sleep. I was barely awake, and I knew it could only be a death in the family or Donna. She was a little hysterical. "Why is this vinaigrette broken? Why didn't you fix it before you left? What am I supposed to do with it now?"

"Donna, it's always going to break overnight. In the morning you always have to reseason it and remix. It's always that way." I was surprised, given how much she knew about more complicated aspects of cooking, that she didn't seem to remember that a vinaigrette is doomed to break, that after a few hours it will always revert to its original incompatible state, vinegar on the bottom, oil on top.

"This is unacceptable. It needs to be perfect and ready to go when I walk in," she said.

"It's my day off, Donna," I said.

Early on, it was clear that we were both attracted to one another and rubbed each other the wrong way. In some ways I was the daughter she never had; in other ways she saw someone young and passionate about her life and career, which stimulated feelings of fear or resentment. For me, she was glamorous, worldly, and sexy in her mercurial way, and also an older sister or mother figure.

Our days in the kitchen could go from fun and companionable to insane within an hour. She'd hired me to replace her, but she'd worked with the same brigade for ten years. Once, I was teaching them some aspect of a new dish and it was clear they weren't really listening. I found Donna in the dining room folding napkins.

"John and Raoul weren't listening in there just now," I said.

"They know what they're doing, I wouldn't worry about it."

"We're going over the new risotto and they need to listen up."

"Cat, they've been cooking risotto for me for ten years. They don't need a lecture from you."

That night at dinner service, she stormed into the kitchen with a return, slamming the dish so hard on the counter the mound of undercooked risotto hopped off the plate and onto the floor. "If you hadn't been spending so much time out in the dining room, Cat, we wouldn't be having these issues! Now learn how to make some fucking risotto, *please*."

⁓

A fishmonger in San Francisco would make the hundred-mile round-trip to Napa to bring his fish to everyone in the valley. He was well respected, also a friend. Donna was notorious for being seized with inspiration, summoning him on a day that was not his regularly scheduled day. He would make the extra trip and she'd carefully inspect each piece, oohing and ahhing, *This salmon is perfect, look at this color, really a nice orange, really fresh*. Then suddenly she would come upon a piece that she felt was inferior, and she would begin to rant. *Look at this terrible cut! Terrible, terrible cut!* And the dealer would raise his voice, defending his fish, and they would go at it, as if this was an ancient, open-air market in Naples, not an upscale fine-dining establishment in Napa. I would look back and forth between Donna and the fishmonger and try to offer my opinion, which mattered not in the least. As they argued on past the point of amusement and ridiculousness, I would reflect on how Donna drove everyone mad, how her diva dramas were what made her both beloved and infamous.

While my relationship with Melissa had been all business, with her the captain and me the first mate of our tiny ship, with Donna it was complicated, operatic. She said I was a diamond in the rough. I could cook my ass off, but was still naive when it came to the finer things in life. Despite my culinary degree, internship in France, and experience at Old Chatham, I was still a plain-talking girl of modest means from Mississippi. It escaped me, for example, that driving Alma's hand-me-down Honda might give the impression that I wasn't making enough at Don Giovanni to afford a decent set of wheels. Donna, eager for the culinary crowd to see she was paying her new executive chef well, pulled some strings and helped me get a good deal on a leased Range Rover. She helped Hannah and me find the right sort of apartment, then furnished it. Later, after Hannah and I split, she helped me furnish and decorate my new apartment and get back on my feet. Donna could be extremely generous.

I was working the usual sixteen-hour days, changing the menu, hatching my olive oil scheme, and overseeing dinner service and the family meal. Everything was coming at me fast. I was the boss of the kitchen, I kept telling myself in some poorly lit corner of my mind. I saw that Donna was determined to groom me, and I tried to will myself to accept the occasional dysfunction that came along with that. I liked California, saw that this was a place where I could set down some roots, but nevertheless felt unmoored, perhaps the natural outcome of packing up my suitcase one too many times.

was on about. It may have had something to do with the fish order. I've repressed this particular tirade. Though it was indistinguishable from all the others, something rose up in me. I quit on the spot. "I'm not doing this anymore," I said.

"What do you mean? It's Christmas Eve. You can't leave on Christmas Eve," she said.

"I'm not leaving, I'm quitting."

I grabbed my knives and busted out through the back door, Donna on my heels, yelling the whole way. It was the first and last time I've ever walked out on a job. I was raised to be on time, work hard, treat your employers with respect, and give proper notice. I didn't believe in quitting because a job proved to be more than you'd bargained for, or because you were tired. But this situation was poisonous, and I needed to get out before I'd absorbed too much of Donna's low opinion of my abilities.

I peeled off, drove around all morning through the Napa Valley mist in that Land Rover Donna had insisted I lease. I'd never leased a car before, and who knew what would happen to it now that I was unemployed. It drizzled a bit. A single run-on thought looped through my head. *I'm done, I'm free! I'm done, I'm free! I'm done, I'm free!* I called my mom and she said, "Thank God and hallelujah." Finally, the mist lifted. It was going to be a crisp, cool Northern California day, and I went home, lit a fire, poured myself a glass of good wine, and wrapped Christmas presents.

I felt I'd excelled in my executive chef position. With Donna and Giovanni's help, I jettisoned that tired old Italian restaurant menu circa 1970 and introduced them to hip, light Mediterranean fare (which they still serve as I write this), helped them create a signature olive oil, and got them on the Net. Still, it had ended so badly I felt a little ashamed.

Not long ago I called Donna. I had heard from a friend that she'd been diagnosed with brain cancer, and I called to see how she was doing. Almost twenty years had passed and I felt my old fondness for her energy and even her histrionics. She had made me a big part of her life, had been generous in so many ways. And she had brought me to California, where I finally set down roots. I owed her a lot, and I was genuinely sorry to hear she was sick.

She caught me up on everything that was going on with the restaurant and our mutual acquaintances in Napa. She was still obsessed with redecorating and replacing the bistro's chairs every other year, and wondered whether I'd had a chance to check out Per Se, Thomas Keller's newest restaurant in New York. Before I could fill her in on what I was doing she said, "I'm just so proud of you, Cat. It doesn't surprise me one bit. You were always so good at showboating."

Showboating.

This wasn't the first time she'd accused me of this—wanting to be out in the front of the house instead of back in the kitchen where she felt I belonged. My impulse was to snap back that I loved being in the kitchen, but it was so much water under the bridge, and I didn't bite.

I wanted to connect with her and felt I had reached a place where I could afford to accept her as she was, backhanded compliments and all. The conversation stumbled a little, then we got to talking about how tough it was to maintain any sort of balance in your life when you worked in the restaurant business. We reminisced about Giovanni, the old crew, and old friends, and the Bistro Don Giovanni olive oil, made from the loose olives that fell in the driveway.

Not long after this conversation I heard she'd died. I felt sadder than I ever imagined I would. Hannah, who still lives in Napa, texted me with the news. At her funeral, her best friend, Barbara, took me aside and said that despite our rocky past, Donna loved me. I felt a sense of closure I hadn't expected. I loved that woman and she drove me mad, and I felt guilty for whatever part I played in our difficult dealings with each other. I was grateful that during our last conversation we seemed to have found peace with each other.

~ fourteen ~

Nothing quite ruins the high of quitting your job than the first overdue bill. It was 1997. I was thirty years old and had no job and no prospects. I'd split from the one person who'd loved me and put up with my shit. I had eight hundred dollars in my savings account. My rent was nine hundred dollars, and it was overdue.

My parents would have starved to death before allowing the thought of unemployment to even enter their heads. "That's one thing you never want to do," my mother counseled me once. I can still see her in the kitchen, pointing at me with a wooden spoon. "Do not go on the dole. You will lose your pride if you start taking from the government."

Three months passed. I spent my days working out, sending out résumés, beating the pavement, then working out some more. Thomas Keller over at The French Laundry was sympathetic to my situation. He offered me an internship, which paid something like $7 an hour, and which I turned down on the spot. I was grateful—also terrified—but I wasn't about to go backward. I drove around up and down the valley in the Land Rover until I couldn't afford the gas. When I was down to a meal a day I gave in and applied for unemployment.

I'd canceled my appointments with Robin the day I quit,

feeling that therapy was the ultimate luxury. After a month or so she called to check up on me, suggesting I schedule an appointment.

"Robin, I don't have a job. I can't pay you."

"I'll tell you what. We can do this. You give me some cooking lessons in trade for therapy."

Robin came to my apartment once a week. We began with roast chicken and talking about why I'd been so susceptible to Donna's charms and manipulations. We moved on to making a stock from the carcass and examining how much of it had to do with the sexual abuse I'd suffered all those years ago. From the stock we made *rivithia*, Greek chickpea and roasted pepper soup, traditionally eaten during Lent, and explored the additional anguish I'd endured when my parents discovered the abuse and more or less let it go.

Some nights I would lie awake and wonder how long I could survive without a job. What would happen to me? I closed my eyes and tried to imagine moving home to Jackson, getting my old job back at the University Club. Was the executive chef who'd taken me under his wing still there? What would he make of my travails? It seemed possible that I might pass out simply from contemplating the potential for humiliation, while at the same time acknowledging that I was getting myself into a state for no reason. I was an experienced chef. I was a *good* chef, and somehow I would make something happen.

One day, when I was about an inch away from destitute, the phone rang. It was Michael Chiarello.

"I hear you're looking for something," he said.

"Yeah," I said. Hope stirred.

"I've got a great restaurant opportunity in the East Bay. You'd be the perfect chef."

I wasn't quite sure where the East Bay was, and I only knew

Michael through reputation. He was a fellow graduate from the Culinary, and the founding chef of Tra Vigre, a restaurant in nearby St. Helena. He was charming and entrepreneurial, had won a slew of prestigious awards, including Chef of the Year by *Food & Wine* magazine and the Robert Mondavi Culinary Award. His new venture would be owned and managed by his restaurant group. I liked the idea of being the executive chef at a restaurant that was not someone's doted upon only child, but purely a business venture.

I searched for quarters beneath the couch cushions and in the pockets of the winter coat I hadn't worn since Old Chatham to put together enough money to buy gas to drive to the East Bay. It turned out I did know where it was—Oakland, Berkeley, all the great little towns east of San Francisco.

The place had formerly been called Tourelle and was a local landmark in Lafayette, California. The town sits among rolling hills covered with wildflowers and scrub. There's a pretty reservoir, a terrific school system, and a well-off populace that enjoys fine dining. Berkeley is just over the hills, due west.

Built in 1937, the restaurant was once Lafayette's post office—hence the new name, Postino, Italian for postman. It was the most beautiful place I'd ever worked, and that was saying a lot. A flagstone walk led up to its atrium entrance, and ivy and jasmine vines grew up the brick walls. Inside there were five or six smaller rooms, also lined with brick, and on the small patio, a few "personal" fire pits around which guests could gather on cool evenings.

The challenge in opening a restaurant there was getting people to come not just from neighboring Berkeley to the west, but from as far away as San Francisco, which would mean a drive across the Bay Bridge and over the hills to Lafayette. But my situation was dire enough that I would have snapped up the job even if it were in a ghost town in the middle of a desert.

It turned out I had no cause for worry. From the time it opened in May 1998, Postino was a hit. I could not have lucked into a better situation. Michael generously offered me profit-sharing, which means that unlike the equity partners, I would receive a portion of the earnings without sharing the risk. Because this time I was a bona fide executive chef, and not in name only, I brought on my own cooks, including my great friend from the Culinary, Lorilynn, the Julia Child–size redhead with the infectious laugh, whom I appointed my sous chef. I'd always been impressed with Lorilynn's organizational skills and also her palate. She's a gifted baker, an expert at classical technique, and her dishes were always both whimsical and satisfying. But more than that, she was like a big sister, the great friend who would always answer the call to go into battle with me.

<hr>

I'd helped open the Sheepherding Co., but Postino was four times as big and located on busy Mt. Diablo Blvd. Everything involved in opening this restaurant was more expensive, more complex.

By now I was experienced and confident enough to have fun with the menu. Crisp onion rings, Meyer lemon and rock shrimp, fried in rice flour with buttermilk and served in a paper cone with spicy mayonnaise. Asparagus with pancetta. Homemade crusty calzone stuffed with prosciutto, sheep's cheese, and truffle oil. Halibut crusted in cheese and served with roasted potatoes and a sweet corn zabaglione sauce. Fresh pulled mozzarella with local heirloom tomatoes. Garganelli pasta rolled by hand with braised rabbit, pancetta, and local wild mushrooms. Michael's connections in the wine industry contributed to a great list of which I was proud.

⁓

Suddenly, life was not just good but great. I was finally an executive chef with no strings attached, making good money. I'd extricated myself from Don Giovanni, and had finally moved on from Hannah. I felt free, suddenly, and filled with a wild joy.

After I left Bistro Don Giovanni, Jean-Pierre, my swashbuckling French partner in olive oil creation, had kept in touch. On those desperate, unemployed nights when I spent hours calculating in my head how I was going to make it through the month, he would take me out to eat. He was gracious enough to pretend that he was starving and I was doing him a favor by joining him. I was so grateful for his friendship, and not unattracted to him, so we started sleeping together. I had had very little experience with men, but the unspoken agreement was always that in exchange for their care and companionship I would try, to the best of my ability, to make them happy. I wasn't turned off, but there were limits. Every time we had sex, I couldn't wait to jump out of bed and move on. There was never any cuddling, secret sharing, or planning for the future. I could only do those things with a woman.

After I'd started at Postino and our fling had played itself out, Jean-Pierre did me another favor by turning Lorilynn and me on to a great place to live. His ex-wife had a huge house, with a lot of empty rooms to rent. She was rarely there, and Lorilynn and I would have the run of the place.

I worked harder than I ever had, and played harder, too. I hadn't been single in eight years and hooked up with pretty much everyone who caught my eye. There were a few servers at Postino, including a lovely guy named Chase, an aspiring opera singer with whom I would remain friends, and a number of avowed straight ladies who were interested in experimenting and felt I was a safe bet. One was Alexa, who was sharp tongued and had a crazy head of curly hair.

Lorilynn was forever rescuing me from situations with chicks that were probably against my better (i.e., sober) judgment. Once I was invited back to an employee party at Bistro Don Giovanni and I invited Lorilynn to come along. Donna and Giovanni were always generous with the alcohol, and the drinks were flowing. Around 1:00 a.m. Lorilynn was ready to leave, and I was nowhere to be found. After searching the dining room and patio, she found me in the kitchen, sandwiched between two hot Latina waitresses, making out in the back of the pantry. She pulled me out by my collar. I stumbled along, throwing kisses back at my new girlfriends and promising to call. She said, "Come on, lover girl, it's time to pour you into bed."

Another night I went out drinking with some friends at a bar in Berkeley, and started flirting with the bartender. She was Italian, funny and sexy, and reminded me of Penelope Cruz. If memory serves, her name was Carmen. Since I was living in this big, gorgeous house, I thought why not invite her over for dinner? I'd never forgotten the blueberry muffins Blake made for me on our first date, and the effect they'd had on me. I set about using all of my by-now top-notch culinary skills to make Carmen a meal she'd never forget.

I pulled out all the stops. Olive oil roasted artichokes with shaved Reggiano cheese. Sliced prosciutto and lightly grilled peaches with a drizzle of rich vincotto. Pillowy potato-truffle gnocchi with fresh summer truffles and light cream sauce, topped with more truffles. Succulent lemon-and-herb-roasted chicken, the juices still running. Fresh pulled mozzarella, still warm and weeping milk, that melted the moment it touched our tongues.

We drank wine and flirted over antipasti, then sat down to a beautifully set table. I was proud of myself for thinking about the table setting ahead of time, because it would have been criminal to break the mood with the need to locate place mats and clean flatware. Did we make it past the second course? I have no memory. What I do recall is the movie moment when I stood up, pulled her up by her hands, swept our glasses and plates to the floor, and pushed her onto the table. I straddled her, and after some desperate kissing and groping, she simply stood up, me with my legs wrapped around her waist, and carried me into the bedroom.

Lorilynn came home a few hours later, very annoyed at the mess we left on the dining room floor, and the moans and cries that issued from my bedroom all night long. That was surely the epic sex of my life, and I wish I could report that Carmen and I had one of those great passionate affairs that come along once or twice in a lifetime. We went out a few more times after that, but it was clear the meal had been more of an aphrodisiac than I'd ever imagined.

⌒

Now that I could pay her, I set up weekly phone appointments with Robin. I gave her the basics of my childhood abuse, and I came to understand the depths of my shame. I remembered things I'd worked hard to forget. How AH said my parents would be disgusted with me if I ever told them what *we* were doing. Meaning, of course, what he was doing to me. He'd used that word, "disgusted." A word so powerful that it stuck. Deep down, I was disgusted with myself. For how many years had I hurled myself into clubs, classes, training, working in an effort to escape this? Cooking, my vocation and life's work, was conveniently physically demanding and all-consuming. I'd do sixteen-hour days in a hundred-degree kitchen and three hundred covers over soul-searching any day of the week, but now it was time to stop and examine the very thing that had driven me all these years: proving that I was good enough.

They say that cooking is love. The love in question might be for earth's bounty, or the perfection required to assure that every plate leaving the kitchen is flawless, or the stamina, discipline, and fortitude required to cook at the highest levels. Maybe it's love for the people you are nurturing with your food, or the ancient, communal experience of breaking bread. Before I began working with Robin, I secretly believed I cooked because without a plate of delicious food to offer someone, I was essentially unlovable.

After our May opening I worked six months without two consecutive days off. Whenever I called home Alma got on the phone and forced me to admit my sixteen-hour days had actually inched upward to eighteen-hour days. After my mom earned her PhD and came back home, no one saw any reason why Alma should leave.

She was ninety-six by then and saw no point in mincing words. I was a fool to work so hard, she said, and to ensure that I would take some R and R she was sending me some money to go visit Lorilynn, who'd just landed a great job on the island of Lanai, in Hawaii. Alma liked to say that her attitude about money was that when her purse was open, it was wide open, but then it slammed shut. Meaning, when she was feeling generous she was very generous. She deemed my exhaustion a crisis, and opened her purse wide. I was bowled over by her compassion. I can be stubborn and disagreeable, but it never

end, I might have been able to talk my way out of it, but
months had passed since Alma's death, enough time for
accept that working every day until I was also in the
wasn't going to bring her back or make my life better, so
ed myself to be persuaded.

drove up in the dark, and when we woke up it was
g too hard to ski. Rather than sit in the condo and
each other, we went to the lodge. At 9:00 a.m. the
ened. The snow came down thicker and faster, creating
ut conditions, so there would be no skiing for the fore-
future. As it was also my birthday, I saw no reason not
myself a Corona Light. The lodge was more crowded
ual, given the bad weather, and I found a spot next to
p, where a couple was seated, a lanky blonde and her
d or husband. Or so I presumed.

heavy snow this late in the season gave the lodge a
ir. I wasn't the only one knocking back beers before
he blonde asked where we were from, and we all got
ng. We ordered another round. I was feeling pretty
d friendly. Damn if that blonde wasn't just my type.
bright brown eyes, an elegant nose, and a dazzling
e was feminine and very pretty, but also looked like a
f substance, one who would give you a run for your
Vas she flirting with me? With her boyfriend or hus-
ng right there?

ly, he pushed back his chair back and excused him-

your boyfriend or husband or whatever?" I blurted

all," she said. "I don't date men."
Neither do I. Are you seeing anyone?"

occurred to me to cross Alma. After ensuring that Max, my sous chef, would be able to cover the restaurant, I bought my ticket, took the shuttle to SFO, and got on the plane.

Meanwhile, back on Swan Lake Drive, someone with good if not well-thought-out intentions had given Alma a swivel chair for her desk for Christmas. For some time Alma had had trouble getting in and out of chairs, and moving them up or away from the table. Alma was overjoyed with her present, went to sit down, the chair seat bobbled beneath her, and she fell, breaking her hip.

I was waiting for my return flight at the Honolulu airport and called home to let my parents know I was getting ready to board. My dad answered, and assuming that I was already home in California, mentioned Alma's fall and that now she was in the hospital.

I got hysterical. I was so far away, and Alma was so old. I stood crying noisily outside the newspaper stand. I wiped my eyes, then saw a familiar face across the concourse: Chase, the server at Postino with whom I'd had a fling, and who'd become a good friend. He was there with his mother, also traveling back to the mainland. He rushed over and took me by the shoulders.

"Cat, hey hey hey, what's going on?" he said.

"It's my grandmom. She broke her hip and she's in the hospital," I blubbered.

"Aw!" said Chase, wrapping me in his arms. "It'll be okay! It'll be okay!"

Why do we always say that when we have no idea what we're talking about?

Alma came through the operation better than her doctors expected. By then a few days had passed and I was back at Postino. I called my mom during a break.

"You don't need to come home," she said. "She's stable and improving. Just call her and say hi and tell her you're thinking about her."

"Mom, I should be there."

"Just wait. She's going to be fine."

My impulse was to go back into the kitchen, tell Max to take over, drive to the airport, and take the first plane out. It was just the sort of thing I would do, but I told myself to stay put. My mom had seen hundreds if not thousands of people at all stages of recovery and decline, and she was sitting at her mother's bedside. Surely she knew better than me. Plus, I'd just returned from a long vacation in restaurant time—a week—and was in charge of service that night. I couldn't up and just leave.

The next day I called Alma during a break. Her heart was old and weak, and I could hear that she was struggling to breathe, and I knew without anyone having to tell me that she was in her final moments. I controlled my sobs enough to tell her what she'd meant to me, that no one had ever loved and supported me the way she had. I was only where I was in life because she had introduced me to the nurturing magic of good food. I told her that when I thought of my best friend, it was the image of her face that came to mind.

I could tell when she'd gone. Just like that, it was clear there was no one on the other end of the line. I sat with the receiver to my ear for I don't know how long. I stood up and closed the door to my office, then exhaled a great gulping sob. I could feel my swollen eyes, my raw throat. My head was throbbing with the sheer exertion of it all. I had known people who had died before—a childhood friend who'd committed suicide, a pair of friends from high school who'd died in a car crash, a boy I'd liked who'd died from leukemia—all tragedies to be

sure, but it was nothing like this. With
I go on?

One thing you can always count
have to eat. You may be barely upright
begins at five thirty. Fish needs to be I
stock made, sauce reduced and deg
food plated. As a partner in Postin
chef, my job was largely managerial.
clipboard and the telephone. But N
that some days the only thing that
ing food. When I emerged from the
he stepped aside without question
started prepping. I julienned carro
in the kitchen that could be cho
midnight, Max placed his hand
"Chef, service has been over for a

Grief is never what you exp
movies and on TV, and then, aft
healing begins. In my experience
a lifetime of open-wound mana
is because of Alma. I miss her e

In 1999 my birthday fell on
Wild-haired Alexa had woun
She's since gotten married, a
Tim, were going skiing at La
they invited me along. I was
dare venture too far away fr
a special brunch menu on S
ing the three-hour drive on
and come back Saturday

week
three
me to
grave
I allow
We
snowi
stare a
bar op
whiteo
seeable
to orde
than us
a two-t
boyfrier
The
festive a
lunch. 1
to chatti
warm an
She had
smile. Sh
woman o
money. V
band sitti
Sudde
self.
"Is tha
out.
"Not a
"Really

"Nope, completely single."

Her name was Jennifer Johnson. She told me she worked as a nanny. Geoff, the man she was with, was her employer, along with his wife, Laura. They had one little girl. Then Geoff returned from the bathroom and looked from her to me and back. "Wow. You guys move fast."

─ fifteen ─

After that snowy, half-drunk morning at the ski lodge at Tahoe, Jennifer and I saw each other every day. We'd fallen in love at first sight, and she gave me things I hadn't even known I'd needed. On our first official date she took me to a toy store. "I can tell you're too serious and need to remember how to play," she said. We adored one another, and that somehow gave us the magical powers to find time for each other even given our breakneck work schedules, her a full-time nanny, me at Postino from an hour before it opened to the day's last floor mop.

Born in Inglewood, southwest of Los Angeles, and raised in the Bay Area city of Fremont, Jennifer has always struck me as the consummate California girl. Her friends nicknamed her Tommy Girl, because she was a tomboy and was crazy for soccer. She played AYSO club soccer throughout high school, and after she graduated was pretty much done with school. She wasn't interested in academics, and after college she worked at Costco for a while before hooking up with a girl who had a young son. She hung out with the little boy and babysat him once in a while and discovered that she enjoyed it. Not long after that she started working as a nanny.

─

There's an old joke I'll try to tell even though Jennifer will say I'm the world's worst joke teller.

What do lesbians call the second date?
Moving day.

About six months after we met (roughly a hundred years in lesbian time), Jennifer and I found ourselves a little one-bedroom apartment in Oakland on Vermont Street. She brought her shepherd mix, Sierra, and suddenly we were just like a lot of same-sex couples in the Bay Area, doting over our furry child. Jennifer was still working as a nanny for Laura and Geoff, and they traveled a lot. She was away as much as she was home, which meant she could handle my sometimes crazy hours.

One day Michael asked me whether I'd be interested in representing Postino at Taste of San Francisco, an annual charity event whose proceeds go toward ending childhood hunger in America. I said hell yes. Because that was the kind of happy I was then. I cannonballed into everything.

I was assigned a spot between two other chefs in the big exhibit hall. The place was crazy packed with chefs, some very famous, some up-and-coming, bartenders in dress shirts, sleeves rolled up, pouring signature cocktails, winemakers, bakers, and pastry chefs. I showed up in my whites, my hair pulled back into a sleek ponytail. I put some yellow tulips in a glass vase on my table to jazz up my station.

I don't recall what I was demonstrating that day, but I remember I thoroughly enjoyed myself. Postino had an open kitchen, and I'd grown accustomed to working in front of people, making conversation as I plated. I liked interacting with folks, and as the daughter of Spiro and Virginia Lee Cora

of Jackson, Mississippi, I was raised to be as polite and conge-
nial as could be.

None of this was lost on Joey Altman, who passed the time
by my table for a quarter of an hour. Joey Altman was another
chef who had six things going at once, a handsome bro who
looked like the president of the fraternity. He'd worked at
Stars, a landmark restaurant in San Francisco back in the day,
and opened Miss Pearl's Jam House, where he wowed the
persnickety San Francisco crowd in the late eighties with his
African- and Caribbean-inspired fare. He played in a blues-
rock band with a bunch of other chefs, and hosted a local
cooking show called *Bay Café* on KRON4, the NBC affiliate.

Not long after Taste of San Francisco I received a call in the
kitchen at Postino.

"Hey, Joey Altman here. I was thinking you'd be good on
the show; why don't you come on?"

"Great." I said.

Like most cooking shows at the time, *Bay Café* had a production budget of about forty-seven cents per episode. I was
required to provide my own food. *Bay Café* was a "dump and
stir" show, no theatrics, rival teams, or time clock. I demonstrated how to make pine-nut-crusted veal scaloppini with
romesco sauce, crisp garlic, and basil, a favorite dish on the
Postino menu.

Until now, I'd never had a burning desire to be a TV star.
Truly I wasn't hyperaware of any food personalities other
than Julia Child, who despite being older than God had just
launched a new show on PBS, *Julia and Jacques Cooking at
Home* with my other culinary heartthrob, Jacques Pépin. Julia
always liked to say that she was first and foremost an educator,
and I saw what she meant. She happened to be very entertaining, but her goal of appearing on television was not entertain-

ment, but to show people how to make great food in their own kitchens.

The task of making a dish in front of a camera turned out to be weirdly and deeply satisfying. The challenge of working with the food, describing what I was doing, and moving around the kitchen set in a way that was both natural and precise, all while striving to be entertaining, was exhilarating. I felt like a unicycle rider who's just discovered she has an aptitude for juggling a peach, a bowling pin, and a chain saw. The experience also conjured up the unalloyed joy I'd felt performing in the Follies in high school, when I'd felt the simple and all-consuming satisfaction of being fully engaged in a production.

When I finished the segment, Joey Altman told me my timing was impeccable. The cameraman said he couldn't believe I hadn't done this sort of thing before. I put some of their compliments down to the simple need to boost the confidence of the talent, but I felt confident enough to request a tape of the episode, which I then shot off to the Food Network, feeling giddy as I addressed the padded envelope and took it to the post office.

The Food Network was still finding its feet back in the late nineties. It had one hit show with Emeril Lagasse, *Emeril Live!* but was still unclear whether there was a big audience for cooking shows, aside from bleary-eyed mothers who'd just put their toddlers down for a nap. The network was scrambling to expand its audience, throwing pretty much every kind of food-related program they could think of against the wall to see if it would stick. There were shows profiling iconic restaurants around the nation and shows that took famous chefs (or, at that time, any chef they could get) to their homeland where they would cook the food they grew up on. There were food news shows and food game shows, and finally, a show starring

Mario Batali, *Molto Mario*. In 1999, only a few weeks before I met Jennifer, *East Meets West*, hosted by Ming Tsai, a Chinese American chef born in Newport Beach, California, won an Emmy, beating out both Martha Stewart and my beloved Julia Child.

The good news for me, an unknown chef from Northern California without my own restaurant, cookbook, or shtick ("Bam!"), was that my tape would not be tossed onto the pile with hundreds of others, waiting for a bleary-eyed unpaid intern to fast-forward through it. The network was actively seeking new talent, and two weeks later, I received a phone call from someone whose name I've clean forgotten, asking whether I wanted to fly to New York to be a guest on *In Food Today*, hosted by David Rosenthal, where "the world's top chefs stop by to share their secrets."

My big draw, as far as I could tell, was being a Mississippi girl, because their earth-shattering idea was to have me demonstrate how to make chicken and dumplings and fried pickles. I assure you that at this juncture I was more than happy to be pigeonholed as a stereotypical southern cook. I was so tickled and grateful I thought my head would twirl off. I convinced the suits who managed Postino to give me a few days off to fly to New York. Wasn't this a fabulous new development for the restaurant? Having their executive chef appear on the Food Network? They were unmoved, but gave me the time off anyway.

I was well into my thirties now, grateful for all of the opportunities I'd had and proud of my accomplishments, but that mind-blowing experience of one thing effortlessly and obviously leading to another, a life free of the feeling of stuttering and false starts, had thus far eluded me.

That began to change. The morning after the *In Food Today*

taping I flew home to Oakland. I walked in the front door and learned the Food Network had already called, asking if I'd agree to four appearances on *Ready . . . Set . . . Cook*. I had no idea what that was, but I couldn't wait to get back on the set.

Food Network had purchased the rights to a British competitive cooking show, *Ready . . . Steady . . . Cook*, where two teams, the Red Tomatoes and the Green Peppers, each comprising a chef and a member of the studio audience, compete to cook a meal in twenty minutes using the basic ingredients found in the average home kitchen. My opponent was Randall Andrews, billed as "Chef to the Stars." If memory serves, he'd worked for Jack Nicholson.

This time, I didn't even make it to the airport before I received another request to audition. On the day of my last appearance, as I was heading toward the elevator, I was approached by a guy in a blue blazer who introduced himself as Bob Tuschman and handed me his card.

"I have a show I think you'd be perfect for. One of the hosts just left, and we'd love for you to come and try out."

"Absolutely, I would love that. Should I be prepared to do anything special?" I imagined a dish starring okra in my near future.

"We don't care. Make a great peanut butter and jelly sandwich. We just want to see how you do on camera."

The Melting Pot was Food Network's catchall ethnic cuisine show. Five sets of chefs rotated through, demonstrating their favorite dishes from Africa and the Caribbean, Eastern Europe, India, the Mediterranean, and Latin America. Upon closer inspection of my résumé, the executives had discovered my roots were as Greek as they were southern and paired me with Rocco DiSpirito, an Italian American, to represent Mediterranean cuisine.

I auditioned in New York and was at Postino when I got the call. I immediately phoned Jennifer. "You aren't going to believe this! I got it! I got it!" I was hyperventilating, the walls of my little office off the kitchen were spinning. I jumped up and down and shrieked and Jennifer jumped up and down and shrieked on the other end of the line, both of us behaving like middle schoolers who'd just found out they'd made the cheerleading team.

My cohost, Rocco DiSpirito, was everywhere in 2000. A few years earlier he'd opened Union Pacific in Gramercy Park, about which restaurant critic Ruth Reichl swooned in *The New York Times*, "Even in New York, where bright young chefs are a dime a dozen, his cooking stands out." He was also coming off of a bunch of best new chef nods from *Food & Wine, Gourmet*, and the James Beard Foundation, and he was more than ready for his star to affix itself firmly in the culinary heavens. As far as show business goes, he had it all: looks, personality, and ambition.

Pilar Sanchez, the show's original cohost, left after the first season, opening the door for me to take her spot on the rickety set off the FDR Highway, bantering with Rocco while whipping up souvlaki, *loukoumathes* (fritters with honey and cinnamon), chicken soup with *trahana* (homemade pasta), *hilopites* (egg pasta with fava bean, feta, and mint stuffing), *keftedes* (Greek meatballs), and for the Mediterranean dessert show, *galaktoboureko,* a simple custard pie.

I was proud of my ability to catch on quickly to the demands of demonstration cooking on television. I privately thought that my background as an all-star softball player, drill team member, and Gayfer Girl had laid the foundation for my easy success. Aside from finally coming into my own as a chef, I was small, nimble, and a quick study.

But next to Rocco, I was as green as could be. I aimed to be as natural as possible, but soon discovered there's *natural*, and then there's *TV natural*. Rocco already understood that the sweet spot for a television chef was the place where serious cooking met absorbing entertainment. He had a dialogue coach and an assistant who counted his lines to make sure that he had the lion's share during any particular show. He liked everything to be scripted, which made me nervous. My ability to wing it was my strong suit and I couldn't imagine saying, "Wow! Look at those gorgeous eggplants, Rocco!" with anything resembling a straight face.

I had nothing but fond feelings for Rocco. He was warm and liked to laugh. He was generous with his advice. After a shoot we'd go down to Blue Ribbon on Sullivan Street and drink martinis. He'd worry like an Italian mother about whether I'd gotten myself a Hollywood agent yet, or when I was going to open my own restaurant.

"You got to learn to schmooooooze, Cat!" he'd say, then laugh.

He was accurate on that point. My life was going to work and coming home in the dark, flying to New York on the red-eye for a solid week of shooting two shows a day, then back on the red-eye in order to open Postino in the morning. In my copious free time, I was trying to make a life with my girlfriend. My hour hanging out with Rocco at Blue Ribbon *was* my schmoozing.

~ sixteen ~

By now the suits at the Food Network had a sense of who I was, that I wasn't just some girl from Mississippi shilling panfried chicken and cornpone but had been raised from the cradle with world-class Greek cuisine that was as exciting as it was healthy.

They signed me up for an episode of *My Country, My Kitchen*, where "top chefs journeyed to their homeland to reveal the flavors, foods, and cultural inspirations that influenced their cooking." Rocco DiSpirito signed on for Italy. Rick Bayless was dispatched to Mexico. Sam Choy did Hawaii. I, of course, went to Skopelos, to film Aunt Demetra and Uncle Yiorgios's annual Greek Easter feast. I'd never filmed on location, and somehow it didn't occur to me that this would be radically different from doing dump and stir in front of three cameras on the Food Network set.

My Greek relatives were overjoyed at the prospect of a visit, especially since my dad was coming along to translate. It had been ten years since Hannah and I had showed up hungry on their doorstep. We had been wayward girls, young and clueless. Even though my Greek was no better now than it was then, I wanted Aunt Demetra to see how I'd turned out, eager to tell her—or have my dad tell her—that I hoped to be able to learn how to cook as well as she did.

My family had agreed to be filmed and knew we were bringing a film crew with us, but when we showed up with dozens of equipment boxes, lights, reflectors, tape recorders, and cameras, they looked horrified. Their son, my cousin Yanni, was a budding attorney and insisted on going over the fine print on the release forms, as if we slick Americans with our shot list and inflexible schedule were trying to pull a fast one. This entailed a solid two hours of discussion-slash-argument in Greek between my dad, Yanni, and my uncle, who as the man of the family was entitled to get into the act as well.

A proper Easter feast demands the roasting of a goat over a spit, and the Karagiozos fire pit has occupied the same spot since the Stone Age. Maybe earlier. We were getting ready to go to Easter church service when the director pulled me aside and said they would need to move the fire pit. Apparently the location of the pit and the backdrop against which the goat would turn wasn't aesthetically pleasing, or the lighting was wrong, or something, and the director asked Uncle Yiorgios if perhaps he could redig the pit somewhere more photogenic. My dad had to translate the request three times to Uncle Yiorgios, because he could not believe the request. What lunatic would ask such a thing? It was impossible.

We stood around in our finery as another two-hour discussion-slash-argument ensued, my dad translating between the director and the Greeks. You could tell whatever thrill my dad had enjoyed from being the translator had run its course. I'm sure he wished he taken the time to teach me Greek when I was a kid and he'd had the chance.

In the end the crew made do with the existing pit, we ate Aunt Demetra's delicious spread, drank some ouzo, and danced for hours beneath the Aegean stars.

This happened many times during our visit: the crew would

complain about something, my family would be mystified, and Dad would be required to step in and break the news that their lifelong traditions did not possess the necessary TVQ. As often as not my family refused to budge, but at five o'clock Greek coffees were offered, then wine and ouzo and many Greek cookies, and finally a decision would be reached and we would do the shoot.

For most of the trip I felt conflicted and agitated. I knew enough about TV production to understand the crew's point of view, but started losing my patience when they would grouse about how late the Greeks ate, or how their towels were thin. They stayed next door, in tourist apartments owned by my aunt. I worried that she would find their petty complaints insulting. I also lost sleep wondering whether in my haste to share my Greek family's culture with the American television-watching public, we were in fact taking advantage of my family's great generosity, but in the end everyone was more or less happy. I was grateful for a once-in-a-lifetime experience to spend Greek Easter with the Karagiozos family, and that year *My Country, My Kitchen* went on to win a James Beard award.

⟶

One day the phone rang and it was an editor from the *Contra Costa Times*, the local East Bay newspaper. She said she'd seen me on *The Melting Pot* and was thrilled to discover that I was local. Would I like to write a column for them? Why yes, I most certainly would, even though I would have to cut into my already precious sleep to do it.

The column was called Cooking from the Hip, and it was so popular the editor hatched another idea: an occasional feature called Chef's Surprise, where I would show up at someone's house with a photographer and an assistant and prepare dinner for the entire family using only the ingredients on hand. The name of the winner was drawn from the hundreds who responded to the paper's call for lucky winners, by which I mean guinea pigs for what at the time was a kooky experiment.

Most people never knew what they had in their pantry. I found it gratifying to show them what they could do with a little creativity and one hour. That was the limit: one hour. On the spot, I improvised ways to cook beans, rice, tomatoes, and more dried herbs than they knew what to do with. My secret weapon was pasta. Even the barest cupboard always seemed to have a box of spaghetti tossed in the back.

Once the winner was an elderly woman who possessed an equally elderly oven that hadn't been cleaned in the last century. I breathed a sigh of relief when I opened her fridge and saw a whole fryer chicken. Not ideal for roasting, but it would certainly do. I slathered it with olive oil and squeezed a lemon over it, then rubbed on cracked black pepper and some herbs. I slid the chicken into that old oven and may have regaled folks a bit with the story of how, when I decided to learn how to cook back in Jackson when I was still living with my parents, roast chicken was the first dish I perfected.

Suddenly, it sounded as if firecrackers were going off. I bent down to peer into the filmy oven window, only to see the chicken and the crud coating the bottom of the oven burst into flames. Luckily my hostess had a little red fire extinguisher stuck in a bracket on the wall. I grabbed it and threw open the oven door. Smoke and flames roared out. I leaned back and doused the chicken and the inside of the oven and stove top.

After we all realized the house wasn't going to burn down, we laughed and decided the experience was pretty entertaining. I was quickly learning that from an entertainment perspective, if a meal can't be spectacular, the next best thing is disaster. It's dramatic, and often demonstrates a useful lesson—in this case the lesson was the importance of cleaning your oven.

⁓

On another day the phone rang and it was a book agent named Doe Coover, wondering if I'd given any thought to doing a cookbook.

"Actually, I have," I said.

Doe Coover specialized in nonfiction, with an emphasis on cookbooks. While shooting *Bay Area Café* I became acquainted with identical twins Mary Corpening Barber and Sara Corpening. They were also regulars on the show, and had just published a book on smoothies. They passed my name on to Doe.

I had long dreamed of doing a cookbook, but had no idea how one went about pursuing it. I knew exactly what it would be—a celebration of the food I'd cooked in all the kitchens of my past: my childhood kitchen in Jackson, my ancestral Greek kitchen on Skopelos, and the best recipes from the kitchens I'd come up in. Doe and I worked up a treatment, and two years later, in 2004, *Cat Cora's Kitchen* would be published by Chronicle Books.

⁓

The phone rang again. This time it was the James Beard Foundation, calling to invite me to cook one of their prestigious dinners. I had to laugh. At first I thought they were only getting around to reading the letter Jacques Pépin had sent four years earlier, on the occasion of the dinner I'd cooked for him at Bistro Don Giovanni, but it wasn't that. They'd seen me on TV, knew I had a cookbook in the works. My star was on the rise.

Cooking at the Beard House was a big deal in 2002, a feather in any up-and-coming chef's toque. Even though there was no application process and you had to wait with fingers crossed to be invited, you were still expected to assemble your own brigade, buy the ingredients, including wine, and pack up your own *batterie de cuisine* and ship it to New York, as well as make a contribution to the foundation. It took months to plan, including several special trips to the Foundation's brownstone in Greenwich Village to familiarize myself with the kitchen.

I presented my Spring Wine Country Dinner on April 23, 2002. I served four appetizers: Hog Island oysters with a wild mustard flower mignonette; tomato croquetti with a cucumber crème fraîche; Napa Valley spring onion and green garlic tartlets; and smoked salmon rillette with polenta crackers.

I then demonstrated how to pull mozzarella. I melted mozzarella curd in a big pan of hot salted water. After draining the water, I began lifting and stretching the now-softened curd with a wooden spoon, repeating until it was smooth and stretchy. Then I formed the cheese into balls and dropped them into a bowl of cold salted water to infuse them with more flavor.

I incorporated the fresh mozzarella into warm asparagus and truffled fonduta toast. I then served a foie gras "sandwich" on brioche, and for the main course, Napa lamb chops *scottadita* with young fava beans and fruited mustard (*scottadita* loosely translates into "burned fingers" in Italian, meaning that the dish smells so divine you can't wait until it cools to pick up a chop and dig in, thus burning your fingers). For dessert I made a rhubarb and strawberry *bomboloni* and olive oil–toasted almond gelato. For fun, I sent everyone home with a caramel apple dipped in chocolate and rolled in nuts, wrapped with a thank-you note and recipe.

167

My parents flew to New York from Jackson, and Jennifer and her parents came from California. Even Rocco showed up to lend his support. After dinner, there was a question-and-answer period. We then broke down the kitchen and all went out to grab a late dinner and toast the success of the evening.

⟶

As I flew back and forth across the country I had plenty of time to wonder whether I was being too greedy in snapping up every opportunity that came my way, and what that might mean—for me personally, for my relationship with Jennifer, and also for my long-term prospects.

There are two kinds of people in the world: those who can sleep on airplanes and those who can't. The former often find themselves snoring the moment the jet starts down the runway, while the latter—*me*—use the time to fret. So much was happening so fast, and yet it couldn't happen fast enough. I always wanted more. Surely there wasn't anything wrong with that. I was as ambitious as any male chef, certainly as Michael, with his endless stream of cookbooks, sustainable farm, and cookware line, or Rocco, with his dialogue coach, line counter, and acting aspirations. Yet I recalled a conversation I'd had recently with a friend, a child development specialist. She was an expert in the psychology of newborn babies. She'd mentioned something in passing that I couldn't shake. If a newborn cries and no one picks her up, one of her first experiences of the world is that she is on her own. Of course, we are all on our own, ultimately. We enter and leave this world alone, but the two-day-old who is picked up and held perceives that it's possible that someone somewhere will have her back. I thought about the week I spent at the Mississippi Children's Home, after I was taken from my birth mom, Joanne, and before I was adopted by my parents. I'm sure people were as good to me as possible, but I feel certain that there were times when I was left to cry, all alone among the other babies. My first thought, even if I had no language for it, was that if I was going to get anything for myself, I and I alone would be the one to do it. Which meant seizing every moment and saying yes to every opportunity that came my way.

The group that ran Postino remained unmoved by my success. Even though every time I appeared anywhere I was introduced or tagged as "Cat Cora, executive chef of Postino," they were unconvinced that the PR they were receiving was more valuable than my ability to expedite. When I would tell them I needed a week off to go to New York to shoot *The Melting Pot*, they sighed and pursed their lips as if I were asking them for time off to go on a cruise. The CEO, the VPs, they were all nice enough guys, but they were never able to grasp that my costarring on a nationally televised show on Food Network was helping put Postino on the map and therefore was good for business.

I learned after a while that they weren't that interested in raising Postino's profile. As long as it raked in the dough, the owners didn't mind if Postino remained a great little village restaurant, beloved by the locals. But I had bigger aspirations for it, for us. I wanted to help elevate Postino to a nationally known eatery.

But gradually I was coming to see that I didn't have the support of the company. They let me go shoot my Food Network shows, but they didn't encourage me to go. The more opportunities that came my way, the more they seemed to disapprove. Conflicts arose. The general manager, whom I'd taken under my wing, turned on me, and one of the sous chefs began lobbying for my position behind my back, presuming I would soon get fired or quit.

I was stuck in an awkward place: Postino was my restaurant, but it wasn't really my restaurant, not in the way that Rocco had Union Pacific, Bobby Flay had the Mesa Grill, or Wolfgang Puck had his mini-empire.

I had never aspired to be a businesswoman, but I knew I had to become one. I had to understand my contracts, to learn to negotiate in my own best interest, to learn what it meant to create and build a company, become a brand, promote it and protect it. I had no idea how one went about doing this; I just knew it had to be done, and I was the only one to do it.

Before I gave my notice I recalled a conversation I'd had with Donna during one of our many arguments: "You know, you're never going to be happy just staying in the kitchen." She'd meant it as a criticism, but I chose to interpret it as a prophecy. My attitude was "You're absolutely right. Just watch me."

On January 15, 2003, I called the CEO of the restaurant group and told him I was giving my two weeks. He was furious, and when I offered to stay longer in the interest of making the transition easier, he declined. The thing that made my blood boil? He acted surprised. He was *shocked* that I'd want to leave. That despite my national TV shows, commercials, endorsement deals, newspaper column and food features, starring gigs at food shows around the nation, James Beard Dinner, and impending cookbook, I still didn't find it an honor and a delight to work my ass off for him and feel penalized for wanting to grow. I had spent five years helping to build and nurture Postino, taking it from a ho-hum space on a busy boulevard to a beloved local eatery with national exposure. I wasn't expecting any credit—it had been part of my job, and I'd enjoyed doing it—but the contempt with which my years of hard work were dismissed was galling.

So I decided to throw myself a big ol' going-away party in Postino's private room, knowing full well that the GM who had turned on me would have to serve the party. I ran up the bill, then stuck Postino with it.

I would be remiss if I failed to mention that I had become pretty full of myself by this time. The turn of the century coincided with the rise of the celebrity chef. The Food Network was getting its mission figured out right about the time Anthony Bourdain's *Kitchen Confidential: Adventures in the Culinary Underbelly* hit the bestseller lists, and the word was out: cooking was sexy. Crazy shit went down in the kitchens of your favorite two-star restaurant. Sex, drugs, and rock shrimp tempura with creamy, spicy sauce. Chefs were no longer lowly service workers, enduring miserably long hours in kitchens hot and cramped enough to cause a prison riot, but rock stars.

Before filming a show, I would put myself on a self-styled "cleanse." I already ate fairly healthy, but I would go religious about not putting anything impure in my body until after the show was shot. Impure is a euphemism for booze. After the shoot was over I'd go a little crazy. I would hit the town for a few martinis, then make the rounds. I'd set up a handful of get-togethers. The culinary world stays up late. I could show up at a chef friend's apartment at 1:00 a.m. and no one would bat an eye.

One time I arrived at a producer's apartment so drunk I couldn't tell whether she had six cats or I was seeing double and she actually had only three. This struck me as hilarious—

cats were everywhere!—and I tripped right over one, falling on my ass. The more the producer scowled, the more I cackled like a hyena, which only amused me more. The producer was pissed, although she got over it, going so far as so ask me to cat-sit a few months later.

~ seventeen ~

I knew Jennifer was The One from that day in the lodge in Tahoe, and I saw no reason why we couldn't have a splashy, romantic courtship, just like any other couple. After we'd been dating for about a year and a half, her nanny job sent her to Paris. I followed along, claiming I wanted to revisit the land of my culinary internship. On her first night off I suggested we check out the Eiffel Tower. The evening was warm and the tower was lit from within and glittered bright gold. I threw open a blanket on the lawn beneath it and broke out some good champagne and Brie. Not a minute after I set out my spread some guys standing around nearby started catcalling us, and I hollered back in my kitchen French to beat it and leave us alone.

Jennifer laughed, amused but also growing less enchanted by the minute. It was late and she was hungry. Once the French guys had moved off, I popped the cork on the champagne and poured us each a glass. We sat back and gazed up at the lights of the tower. At 11:00 p.m. the nightly light show began, and as the lights began to sparkle and dance, I asked her, in French, to marry me and produced the ring I'd been nervously fingering in my pocket for hours.

She said *oui*.

We kissed, knowing this was a great beginning to our life

together. On the way back to the hotel, in anticipation of some serious champagne-fueled lovemaking, we stopped at a phone booth and called everyone we knew. It was a glorious night, despite our eleven-hundred-dollar phone bill.

Even though we could only be domestic partners in California at that time, on June 30, 2001, we had a wedding with a capital W at Tre Vigne in Napa. Both of us were beautiful brides in white gowns and delicate veils, with a flower girl, a proper wedding party, and 125 guests.

Our families were all for it, give or take a relative or two who thought it was all right that we were gay—they had no problem with *that*—but why did we have to parade it around by being so celebratory and public and, well, *straight* about the whole thing? Couldn't we just live together and keep it to ourselves, like a couple keeping an illegal cat in a pet-free apartment?

When I left my job at Postino the official response was "Don't let the door hit you in the ass on your way out." I had an insane range of things keeping me busy. A production company in San Francisco had contacted me about developing my own show, and my first cookbook, *Cat Cora's Kitchen*, was coming out in the fall. I'd followed Rocco's advice and gotten an agent at William Morris. Endorsement deals for stuff I'd never even heard of came my way weekly.

My first commercial was a big one, for Johnson & Johnson. Saran Disposable Cutting Sheets. They paid me more money than I'd ever seen in my life. It was the summer after I left Postino, and I was doing a stint at Chez Panisse for fun and to keep my skills up. In those days any chef who dared to do a commercial was considered a sellout, and I knew some of the purists at Alice Waters's place were making comments about me behind my back. One of the servers, who despised hypocrisy, pulled me aside and told me that every female chef in the industry—even some of the gals looking down their noses at me—had auditioned for that commercial, but I was the one who'd landed it. I had a bit more spring in my step after that. Plus that huge payday.

Even good money from Johnson & Johnson wasn't going to last forever. I took a lot of meetings, but a great meeting does not pay the electric bill.

Sometimes I wondered what in the hell was I thinking? Here I was, a trained chef with a good résumé who left a good full-time job at a well-respected restaurant to *build my brand*, a nebulous task if there ever was one. One of the great satisfactions of being a chef is that the work is tangible and obvious. That pile of onions has either been chopped or it hasn't. The stock has been started or it hasn't. The three-top at station six either has received its appetizers or it hasn't. I was trained and wired to work merciless hours tackling what was directly in front of me.

Now my project was launching a chef named Cat Cora. Who was she? Female, first and foremost. Even at the turn of the century the top chefs were overwhelmingly male. Sure, there were Julia, Alice, Anne Rosenzweig, and Melissa Kelly, but they were outliers. Mostly, women were welcomed only in the world of pastry, where the work was precise, calm, and measured, the environment controlled, the ingredients sugar and spice and everything nice.

Cat Cora was a cook and she could cook as well as the boys. Petite and pretty, but not so petite and pretty that she didn't look like she could command a kitchen. Determined and tough, but not so determined and tough as to make her appear unfeminine. Small but mighty was how she played it. She possessed a background people found intriguing, and when she quipped that she grew up eating grits and feta, folks were charmed. Over the years a mistake would be perpetuated that both her father and grandfather had been restaurateurs. It was my godfather, Taki, who was a chef and restaurant owner.

I had managed to charm some key individuals. But charm doesn't pay the mortgage. I called my agent as many times a week as I dared. I let it be known at the Food Network that I was game for anything, was available to fly to New York at the drop of a hat. They took me at my word. Some executive would call and ask to see me as soon as I could get there. I'd race back to Manhattan to do a bunch of auditions, and when time after time I was cast in shows that everyone believed would be big hits but wound up falling flat, I wondered if *The Melting Pot* had been a fluke, and whether it was hubris seasoned with a little insanity that made me quit my regular paycheck job.

Tell you what: I wasn't feeling so full of myself now.

But I was never despondent for very long. Rejection increased my focus, caused me to dig in my heels. A chef's training also confers the habit of never dwelling on failure. I kept on. Just you wait, everyone who'd said thank you but no thank you.

Finally, I was hired to cohost a show called *Kitchen Accomplished,* where a team of kitchen experts—designer Wolfgang Schaber, contractor Peter Marr, and I—would collaborate on a remodel for a lucky homeowner whose kitchen needed renovation. *Kitchen Accomplished* was a hybrid cooking show and home improvement show, where my main job was helping select the big-ticket appliance items, plus smaller but no less important kitchen equipment like knives and cutting boards, bantering with my colleagues all the while. Even though there wasn't much cooking involved, I dug it. I immersed myself in the experience, trying not to pay attention to the reality of the situation: the Food Network had ordered thirteen episodes, but as the weeks passed they failed to order any more.

Looking back, there's no doubt that my ongoing freak-out was due in part to the fact that Jennifer and I had decided it was time to start a family. Not long after we married we bought a town house in the town of Fairfield, equidistant from San Francisco and Sacramento, and less than twenty miles from Napa. I was thirty-six—tick-tock, tick-tock—and if Jennifer and I were going to have the big family of our dreams—we agreed that four was the perfect number of children—it was time to get on it. With that in mind, Jennifer legally changed her last name so we and our future children would all be Coras.

We considered adoption first. I was the poster girl for successful adoption, managing to maintain a close relationship with both my adoptive family (whom I just thought of as my family, period) and my birth mom. Jennifer and I set out to find an agency to help us. We interviewed at least a dozen, and to a one they were all encouraging until the moment they learned that Jennifer and I were not sisters or friends, but wives. Every single agency turned us down flat.

I had a romantic notion that the Mississippi Children's Home, the agency that had placed me with my parents thirty-six years earlier, would be open to helping us. They were solely responsible for placing me with wonderful people, and I was sure they would want to continue the legacy. The social worker I spoke to first was delighted to hear from me, the famous hometown girl who'd made good, calling to adopt. Of course they could help me! When I told her the situation, that I was gay, she was hesitant, but still open. When I told her I had a wife, she said absolutely not. I was hurt and mystified; a single gay woman could adopt, but not a married couple? It still breaks my heart to think that one of those kids could have been ours.

We started to explore in vitro, which would require a donor. Before we even settled on the right sperm donor bank we were stricken by the responsibility of being placed in the position of deciding on the other half of our future children's DNA. The sperm bank we used gave us a dossier of profiles, which we pored over for months. The donors were mostly med students at UCLA and Stanford, who'd aced organic chemistry or quantum something or other. Obviously, most would-be parents in search of a donor wanted to do their best to ensure their kids had some smarts. But we were also interested in physical features, religious belief, and appetite for world travel. We went through one insane week when we thought we should know the donor's favorite color. Finally, we decided on a smart, seemingly attractive Greek American (we had no pictures of the donors, only physical descriptions), a painter and an athlete who'd traveled and whose ambition was to finish medical school and do research in genetics. Even more appealing to us, he had, according to the sperm bank, retired from the donation business. We wanted our children to feel as though they belonged to us and weren't part of a huge tribe of half brothers and sisters roaming the planet. This apparently was a common attitude, because the bank had a policy that once you gave birth using one of their donor's sperm, you could buy the rest. After our first son was born, we bought every vial of the donor's sperm and took them to our OB-GYN. This nameless, faceless donor is the biological father of all of our children. Our boys call this man their "sperm dad," and we are endlessly grateful to him, whoever he is.

Jennifer retired from nannying and set about trying to get pregnant. It wasn't simply a matter of dusting off the ol' turkey baster. Her doctor put her on Clomid to induce ovulation every month, and also monitored her ovarian follicles with ultrasounds at regular intervals. The Clomid made her feel nauseated and pregnant without actually being pregnant. She decided she needed something to occupy her time and offer some distraction, so she applied to help with the grape harvest at Stag's Leap in nearby Napa, where she learned about winemaking, from picking grapes to corking the bottles. While she was spending her days learning how fermentation works, I was manically taking meetings, appearing at festivals, conferences, and events, and doing everything I could to launch my brand. After I gave notice at Postino, it didn't escape my notice for a single day that I had no steady work, and soon, a baby on the way.

After six or seven months Jennifer conceived, and gave birth to our first child on October 24, 2003, a beautiful boy we named Zoran. Jennifer took to motherhood easily. Maybe it was all those years working as a nanny, coupled with her calm temperament. Whatever physical traits the sperm dad's DNA contributed were not readily apparent at birth. Zoran was dark-eyed, with well-proportioned features and a mouth shaped just like Jen's.

Holding our baby in my arms for the first time, I was struck by the realization that it wasn't about me anymore, and that I was responsible for this helpless little being, a being who was largely unknown, with whom I fell immediately in love, and for whom I would lay down my life.

⌒

Later that year, while on a book tour for *Cat Cora's Kitchen*, I received a call from Bruce Seidel, an executive producer at the Food Network. This was nothing out of the ordinary. They called me all the time for pie-in-the-sky shows that never panned out.

After identifying himself he asked, "So, do you want to be our first female Iron Chef?"

"Uh, yeah!" I said, after thinking carefully for a quarter of a second. I figured this was a preliminary chat, and I would be asked to come in and audition along with every other female they knew who'd ever donned chef's whites.

"Great. Your first battle is in two weeks."

"You just want me to—"

"Two weeks," he said.

⌒

Iron Chef (*Ryōri no Tetsujin*, translated literally as "Ironmen of Cooking") was a hit show in Japan in the nineties. No mere televised timed cook-off between competing chefs, *Iron Chef* also had a fictional history. The story went like this: Takeshi Kaga, the so-called Chairman, dreamed of this competition, set in a kitchen stadium that was part of his castle. Chefs from around the globe would come to wage battle against the reigning Iron Chefs of his Gourmet Academy. When the Food Network picked up the show in 1999 and dubbed it into English it became a cult hit, a crazy, entertaining cross between high-octane cooking competition and a kung fu movie.

Inspired by the success of the dubbed original, UPN pro-

kitchen—there truly wasn't time to focus on anything but the task in front of you—but I saw that Kerry had taken that tack as well. After filming began, no one was supposed to leave the set, but at some point in the proceedings Bill Murray slipped out for a walk. Twenty minutes later he returned with a handful of plastic packets of ketchup and mustard, walked right onto the set and into Kerry's kitchen, and slipped them to Kerry.

I lost by 0.1 percent, the slimmest margin in *Iron Chef* history. Was the perfect, charming detail of Bill Murray delivering condiments the reason behind Kerry's one-tenth of a percent win? I'm saying yes. There were no hard feelings in any case. Kerry is a great guy and, well, Bill Murray is the man. It was an honor, no matter what went down.

Battle Clam, against Sam Choy. I beat him by almost ten points. In fairness, I think he shot himself in the foot with his clam flan. I learned from his mistake: never mix fish with anything sweet. It was simply too nasty.

Battle Ostrich, against Walter Royal. He beat me by eight. Ostrich is a protein I find so revolting and despise so hardily that the moment the ingredient was revealed I should have just downed my ouzo and shaken the hand of my competitor. And don't get me started on ostrich *eggs*.

All along the way there were missteps, some more entertaining than others. Stoves failed, fires started, some chefs cut themselves so badly the on-set medic was called in. In one battle, Bobby Flay almost electrocuted himself. Once one of my sous chefs turned on the blender without putting on the lid and the avocado puree spewed all over the counters, the floor, his face.

duced *Iron Chef USA* in 2001. Its two episodes were shot in the MGM Grand Hotel in Las Vegas, with William Shatner cast in the role of the mad, visionary Chairman. The show flopped, due to any number of reasons: a loud, rambunctious Las Vegas audience who behaved as if they were watching a boxing match; commentators who made no effort to look knowledgeable about food cracking endless dumb jokes; the inability to translate the quirky tone of the original.

Undeterred by the failure of *Iron Chef USA*, in 2004 the Food Network produced a four-part miniseries, *Iron Chef America: Battle of the Masters,* introducing a new story line. The Chairman dispatched his "nephew" (martial arts actor Mark Dacascos) to continue the tradition in the United States, where he founded a new Gourmet Academy.

Battle of the Masters, hosted by Alton Brown, with floor commentary by Kevin Brauch, was a hit, and the network then went on to order a full, season-long weekly series. The producers had managed to capture the perfect blend of camp and serious cooking. As in the original show, the contest between the challenger and the Iron Chef involved cooking five courses in an hour, each course featuring a "secret" ingredient revealed by the Chairman at the top of the show.

When I got the call there were only three American Iron Chefs: Bobby Flay, Mario Batali, and Masaharu Morimoto. I was fully aware I was their token female, but I was not about to pass this up. I knew the show had been a huge hit in Japan and featured intense cooking battles that verged on athletic competitions. It was wacky and cool, and I felt in my bones it was going to be big.

My first battle was against Alex Lee, executive chef at DANIEL, Daniel Boulud's flagship fine-dining establishment on the Upper East Side. I was so nervous I could feel my heart beating in my ears, but my attitude was *Bring it on.* I'd brought Lorilynn along as my sous chef. Who knew better than Lorilynn how I worked?

Alex and I stood on either side of the secret ingredient "altar," and when they hoisted up the cover, so much dry-ice fog poured out that for several long seconds I couldn't see anything. The ice was there for dramatic effect and also to help disguise some of the production necessities, like cables and lights. I batted away the fog and saw . . . potatoes. Mounds of russets and red potatoes, ruby crescent fingerlings, yellow Finns, and purple Peruvians. From the moment the ingredient was revealed until my sous chefs and I toasted with ouzo after we'd plated our five dishes, everything was a blur. Battle Potato was slightly more memorable because it was my first.

Chaos did not even begin to describe it. I threw some ouzo into a pan and nearly singed off an eyebrow. One of Alex Lee's ovens went down and he ran over to ask whether he could borrow mine. Then one of my ovens malfunctioned and I ran from my kitchen around the cameraman to use Lee's one working oven, now empty, the metal tray burning my hand through the dishcloth. Someone yelled the time. The fog swirling around my ankles was distracting and crazy-making. Suddenly the plating began. I plated the duck, but I despised it. The sauce I'd made for it looked as if it had been spooned on by a prison cook. It needed something. To be drizzled with a squirt bottle? Maybe puddled, then "smeared" with the back of spoon? Maybe I should slice the duck and fan it out, rather than just plunk it down at six o'clock on the plate? Maybe I should use some micro greens or corn shoots for more color?

With no time left, I started again, slicing, smearing, and opting for both the greens and the corn shoots. I didn't love it,

but I knew it was good. When we were done, I poured shots of ouzo for my team and we toasted and drank up. *Opa!*

I won by one measly point, and damn if it didn't feel good.

I didn't always win, obviously. My next battle was against "rock 'n' roll chef" Kerry Simon, a fellow CIA grad, who had his own place in Vegas and sported a snarly hairdo that wouldn't look out of place in a heavy metal band. Bill Murray was in the audience that day. He knew Kerry from a pizza place they had both worked at in suburban Chicago.

The secret ingredient was actually only semisecret. A few days ahead of filming, the producer would give us a short list. It might be lamb, octopus, butter, or peas. This was helpful, obviously, but we still needed to conceive of five dishes for three or four potential ingredients. My strategy was to choose a cuisine, so that when the ingredient was revealed my team would immediately have a general idea of our direction.

When the ingredient was apples, for example, I knew that every dish would be prepared in the manner of Asian/French cuisine. If the ingredient was oysters, we would go French/Cajun. I would instruct my sous chefs on the pairings in advance. By selecting the type of cuisine ahead of time, the cooking options would be automatically limited, and also create cohesion in the menu. This relieved my sous chefs and me of wasting precious time trying to figure out whether the dishes "clashed" with one another, and also we'd know right out of the gate the flavor profiles we'd be creating. Deciding the style before the secret ingredient was revealed saved a lot of time, and allowed us to focus.

That day, in my battle against Kerry Simon, the secret ingredient was hamburger, and our strategy was global street food. I rarely paid attention to what was going on in the other

Battle Pork, against LA chef Neal Fraser, was a calamitous episode. It should have been called Battle Five Hundred Pounds of Pig. The secret ingredient lid ascended into the rafters, the fog rolled away, and there was an entire hog, nose to tail.

The production schedule was brutal. They often shot all twenty-six episodes in just three weeks, which meant shooting two or three episodes a day. This particular episode began filming around six or seven o'clock. I knew how to break down an animal, and a pig would take at least an hour. When they realized they hadn't removed the spine, they had to stop filming and wheel the pig back down to the butcher. We didn't get started until 9:00 p.m.

Everyone was exhausted. This was *entertainment,* not the Red Cross airlifting rice into Burundi. No one was going to suffer if we bagged it for the night, and yet we had a schedule to keep. We were cranky and miffed, and one of my sous chefs accidentally turned the oven up to five hundred degrees and burned the pork skewers. It was too late by the time I discovered it and I had to go with it. I got good and spanked by the judges and I completely deserved it.

In season three I lost to Walter Scheib, who'd been the White House chef for the past eleven years. I couldn't compete with his sheer expertise. Every day he was making dishes most of us hadn't given a thought to since culinary school. High-end, highly technical dishes for the likes of Nelson Mandela and Václav Havel, and every other dignitary and ruler of the free world. He simply executed better than I did. There was nothing for it.

Bobby, Mario, and Morimoto all ran busy New York restaurants. When the honchos at Food Network would summon them to the studios in Chelsea to film, they'd round up their sous chefs and head on over. Sure, they'd have to create a menu on the fly, but otherwise it was pretty much like an average day in their own restaurants, only with cameramen and dry ice.

It wasn't like I could just go out and buy myself a restaurant as if it were an SUV. Opening a restaurant requires a lot of thought and consideration and financial backing. My time was consumed by flying back and forth across the country for *Iron Chef*, and also guest-starring spots on other Food Network shows. *Cat Cora's Kitchen* was published in 2004, and I was traveling to promote that. I'd started getting endorsement offers for commercials, and spokesperson jobs for big companies like Johnson & Johnson, Sears, Hunt's, Pillsbury, and Kraft. I scored a lucrative gig selling garbage disposals for InSinkErator, which would be the biggest paycheck I had ever seen. My life was busy. My life was fast. I was cooking a lot, but it was on the road: charity events, festivals, food shows.

To open a restaurant requires building a business plan, pondering your concept, finding and courting investors. The logical place for me to open a restaurant would have been somewhere in the Bay Area, Oakland perhaps, or in Napa or Yountville. But I wasn't home long enough to even unpack my bags. I lived in Fairfield with Jennifer and my infant son, Zoran, but in 2005, the year I became an Iron Chef, I simply wasn't settled enough. Timing is everything in life, and this just wasn't the right time.

Because I didn't have my own restaurant, I had to assemble different teams of sous chefs for each battle. It was like going into the NBA finals with a pickup team. I'd try to use my old friend Lorilynn as much as possible, but she couldn't always drop everything and come to New York. I think I won as often as I did because of the generosity of Morimoto, whose own flagship restaurant was within walking distance of the studio. He invited my fledgling team and me to practice cooking together in the mornings before his own chefs arrived for service.

Molecular gastronomy was all the rage in the mid-aughts. Transparent ravioli. Mango foam. Greek salad granita. All the cool kids were turning anything they could into a powder, gel, or jelly. I called Wylie Dufrense, a pioneer in molecular gastronomy and chef-owner of wd-50, one of those places where during dinner service most days you'd see town cars and stretch limos double-parked in front, and he agreed to give me some lessons. The judges were wowed when you put something in front of them that involved, say, liquid nitrogen, and I knew I needed it in my arsenal. It was time well spent: my truffle foam consistently drew raves.

⁓

I'm constantly reminded that I am the first *female* Iron Chef. How extraordinary it was made to seem, that I, a mere woman, had made it into Kitchen Stadium! If I ever battled another woman—and I did on five occasions—the script called for mentioning our gender every fifteen seconds if possible.

It's ladies' night! Have at it, sister! Let's see who emerges victorious in this all-female food fight! On Battle Ricotta, I cooked against Julietta Bellesterous, chef-owner of Crema, and it was apparently necessary to seat three female judges. "Now for some real entertainment," quipped Alton Brown after we'd finished our dishes. "Me and three women eat some cheese!"

Early in my tenure I'd brought on Elizabeth Falkner as one of my sous chefs, and she was invited on to challenge me the next season. They billed it as a girl fight, my sous chef coming back, gunning for me, going against her mentor. They couldn't get enough of the "catfight" jokes.

I was immune to the trash talking, but what got to me if I let it was the reality beneath the spectacle: there was only room for one female Iron Chef, and if another woman beat me, the odds were good she would replace me. After I lost a battle I could be a pain in the ass. I would demand an explanation of the scoring. I was more emotional. I had more at stake.

The male Iron Chefs' (how ridiculous that sounds) battles had a sporting feeling about them. Oh sure, they cooked their asses off. I'm not suggesting Bobby didn't take it seriously or that Mario didn't want to win, just that nothing but their egos was at stake. They weren't battling for their livelihoods.

In the culinary world women are more welcome now than they were in Julia's day—almost no one took Julia seriously as a "real" chef—but what remains unchanged is the way we are, at all times, in a position of having to prove ourselves. We're constantly being pointed out as some adorable or charming anomaly.

My battles with other females were actual battles. After I beat Elizabeth Falkner, I came upon her in her dressing room sobbing. Alex Guarnaschelli, chef de cuisine at New York's Butter (who in 2012 would go on to win *The Next Iron Chef* on her second try), was so nervous during Battle Farmer's Market she misheard the instructions and failed to use all the required ingredients.

Mary Dumont, my competitor in Battle Milk and Cream, confessed that for weeks before our showdown she'd had my picture as her laptop wallpaper, and every time she passed it during the day she would stop and say, "I'm taking you *down*."

In that battle, I busted out a menu that I remain proud of to this day:

Bacalao Soup with Milk and Garlic Cod

Cardamom Milk with Duck Prosciutto Salad, Taro Chips, and Date Quenelle

Spiny Lobster in Saffron-Vanilla Bean Milk, steamed in Fata Paper

Couchon de Lait with Pork and Queso Fresca Ravioli

Milk and Cookies with Bourbon Spiked Milk and Trio of Homemade Cookies Deconstructed: Oreo, Nutter Butter, and Fig Newton

I also threw in a delicious beverage for good measure: Dreamsicle Snow Cone with a Grape Anise Flavor Squirt.

I won 51–46.

⁓

Off camera, my sense of alienation mounted. I never forgot Rocco's directive from my first days on *The Melting Pot*, that I had to learn how to schmooze. The part he neglected to mention—or most likely didn't even know to mention, being a handsome white guy—is that schmoozing isn't like pole vaulting. You can't do it alone. And the environment you're in has to be conducive to schmoozing.

How many times did I attend a get-acquainted gathering only to find that my fellow chefs, as well as the executives at the network or production company, already knew one another? At one cocktail party to kick off something or other, I arrived at the restaurant to find my costars were already bro-ing it up, buying one another drinks and calling each other and our bosses by their last names. Had they already grabbed a few beers before the event? Caught a play-off game or gotten a poker game going? Whatever it was, I wasn't invited, and typical for the token female: you're invited but not included.

My relationships with women in power were also complex. They fell all over the guys. Isn't he adorable/charming/funny/oh so cute? The camaraderie they shared with the guys was based on mild flirtation and flattery. In particular there was a woman high up on the food chain at Food Network who was gay, but never took to me. I knew she would go out with some of the other talent, but never with me. Maybe I was too out and that made it awkward for her? I never expected anything special because I'm gay, but I could have used some support from someone who knew what it was like to be gay and struggle.

⁓

Every time I started taking something like *Iron Chef* too seriously, something would remind me of the true scale of things, of what really mattered. In August 2005, Hurricane Katrina decimated not just New Orleans and Mississippi. The storm made landfall in Buras, Louisiana, and then turned and headed north at the mouth of the Pearl River. For seventeen hours hurricane winds pummeled the coast, spawning eleven tornados and a twenty-eight-foot storm surge and fifty-five-foot sea waves. Every Mississippi coastal town was flooded by at least 90 percent, and every county was declared a disaster area. Jackson is in the central part of the state, and while it suffered eighty-five-mile-an-hour winds—which caused a lot of tree damage, downed power lines, and tore off roofs—my family escaped harm, as did the house on Swan Lake Drive.

Mississippi is the poorest state in the nation. One bright, moneymaking spot had been the Gulf Coast, with its resorts and floating casinos. It suffered near-total obliteration within a seventy-seven-mile-wide swath. Gulfport, gone. Biloxi, gone. My heart, broken.

Ten months earlier, the catastrophic Indian Ocean tsunami had struck. I couldn't stop thinking about how in a matter of minutes people who didn't have a lot to start with lost everything. In response to this disaster, I'd founded Chefs for Humanity, an organization devoted to addressing world hunger. As chefs, our lives are devoted to making great food and feeding people well. Shouldn't part of that work also include providing food for people who don't have enough, or anything, to eat? My parents had always viewed Thanksgiving as an opportunity to feed neighbors, friends, and acquaintances in need. I could hardly stand by and do nothing.

Part of CFH's mission includes emergency relief, and after Katrina I rallied some chef friends and we headed to the Gulf Coast. Fellow southerner Tyler Florence heeded the call, as did Ming Tsai.

Few flights were coming in and out of Jackson; roads were washed out or closed due to downed power lines. We flew in to Jackson and drove to Gulfport. Because we partnered with law enforcement there, we were allowed past the roadblocks.

In Gulfport the tidal surge penetrated a full half mile inland from the beach. Everything behind the surge line was smashed or wiped away. At the surge line mountains of debris formed the highest elevation in town, perhaps in the entire state. Trees pulled up by their roots, splintered wood, broken windows, entire roofs, chunks of pavement, and dozens of cars, which looked like shiny toys dropped from the sky by the hand of God. Local officers couldn't even recognize the streets because nothing was left but rubble.

The Red Cross found an elementary school cafeteria we

could use to cook for local citizens as well as the emergency relief teams and law enforcement. Our kitchen hummed 24/7, producing three thousand to five thousand meals a day. We tapped local chefs to be our sous chefs, and rounded up every other person who could scramble an egg.

The food came from the refrigerators and walk-ins of local restaurants around the area. The structures had been obliterated, but somehow many kitchens escaped. The owners hired refrigerator trucks and brought their food to us. Gulfport had been a resort town and we had everything: lobsters, crab, expensive cuts of beef, burger, pizza dough, pounds of shredded cheese and tomatoes, bushels of lettuce wilting in the heat. We had literally tons of food. The challenge was figuring out how to use it efficiently, to create nourishing, comforting dishes for exhausted, traumatized people.

We bunked in a local Motel Six, miraculously still standing. They gave us three rooms and we drew straws for the beds. The rest of us got pallets on the floor. No one slept, exhausted as we were; it was Mississippi at the dead end of August with no air-conditioning. We had a few window fans, which served only to blow around the mosquitoes. Mostly, we lay in the dark and talked and compared notes about great meals we'd eaten. Chefs to the end.

⌐ eighteen ⌐

I stood in an airplane bathroom on my way to somewhere. Maybe to New York to shoot *Iron Chef.* Perhaps I was out promoting the new cookbook. Or headed somewhere or other to participate in an auction or event for Chefs for Humanity. Could have been to meet with the editors and writers of *Bon Appétit*, where I'd been named executive chef. Or a food festival or trade show. Guest appearance on one of the other Food Network shows. (Iron Chefs were often asked to appear as guest stars.) Very possibly I was on my way to voice a role in a new video game, *Iron Chef America: Cuisine Supreme.*

I was traveling about two hundred fifty days a year in 2008, and this was one of those days. I peeled down my jeans and propped my hip on the edge of the sink. I plunged a syringe loaded with Follistim into the top of my ass and winced. I was forty-two, and if I was going to have a baby the time was now. I couldn't put it off a moment longer. So there I was in a tiny lavatory, my syringes rolling around the counter, the jet engines roaring in my ears.

When Jennifer and I decided we wanted to spend our lives together and start a family, I was already what the doctors call an "older mother." (Thanks, Doc!) We knew we were going to have to get creative to have the kids we'd hoped and prayed for. While I was in my thirties our doctor retrieved some of my eggs and fertilized them with the sperm from the donor we'd used for Zoran. Jennifer carried my biological son, Caje, who was born in 2007 (he's the spitting image of my birth mother's father), and now Jennifer and I were each going to be implanted with embryos created from the other's eggs. Neither of us was getting any younger, and we thought we might as well have two babies in diapers at the same time. Creative, like I said.

The more I traveled, the more hotel rooms in name-your-city I found myself in, the more precious my memories of growing up on Swan Lake Drive became. I didn't have a fancy childhood, but I could bring myself to the edge of tears remembering all us kids—my brothers and me with various friends—in the game room with its pool table, foosball table, and wood-burning stove, jigsaw puzzles in progress on a card table. In the summer the screen door let in the throaty chirps of frogs and hum of night insects, the smell of warm freshly mowed lawn. I was desperate for my own kids to have a chance to live that simple life, to know their grandparents. I wanted to watch them race around in baggy shorts and T-shirts stained with Popsicle.

I was now as ready as I ever would be, so I locked myself in airplane bathrooms to make sure I stayed on shot schedule for my upcoming try at in vitro.

The first procedure took, a small miracle given my age. For three solid days I was euphoric, walked around with my hands on my flat belly, as if I could feel the embryo growing. I would bounce three-year-old Caje on my hip and imagine him with a little sister or brother, no longer the baby. I was thrilled to begin the journey.

Jennifer was a genius of childbearing. Her birth experience was no more taxing than a minor dental appointment.

She'd driven herself to the hospital to give birth to Caje, and the next afternoon went to the bank to pay our quarterly taxes.

But I miscarried after three days. I couldn't hide my disappointment from Jennifer or the boys. I lay in bed with my arm crooked over my eyes and sobbed to the point of dehydration. I was bereft, and also frustrated that no matter how hard I worked, pushed, planned, battled, I couldn't control this. I ate well, exercised, took care of myself, and still my body could not be forced into cooperating.

In the meantime, Jennifer conceived. Again. Her fertility goddess routine was amazing and a little annoying, truth be told. But then, after my doctor cleared me, I got pregnant again. Jennifer was due in April and I was due in July. It would be practically like having twins, we reasoned, and when I went back to work, as I would surely have to ASAP, as our household of six was not going to support itself, Jennifer could breast-feed both boys.

You read that right. Two more boys. Four sons under six, two of them three months apart. The great blessing of my life. Also, are you fucking kidding me?

Being pregnant together drew Jennifer and me closer than ever. After Caje was born we'd moved to Santa Barbara, into a midcentury house painted French butter–yellow, with white shutters and a little palm tree in the front yard. It was on a mesa overlooking the Pacific, on a block where kids could ride their bikes and skateboard, and the neighbors invited each other over for barbecues. At night, after Zoran and Caje had been put to bed, Jennifer and I would sit shoulder to shoulder on the couch, our increasingly swollen feet up on the coffee table, and compare notes on cravings, funny dreams, aches and pains, weird noises rising from our bellies, all that squirming. Privately, I worried about what would happen when we were both ready to pop. Who would lift the heavy boxes? Who would make the midnight runs to the grocery store? Who would tell the other one there was no need to freak the hell out? That had been my role when Jennifer was birthing our sons. Now that I was on the same side of the seesaw, I often wondered how we would manage.

I had no doubt I could continue to work throughout my pregnancy. I was in great shape, and especially after my three weeks cooking in Gulfport after Katrina, had grown to feel "iron" in pretty much every area of my life. My *Iron Chef* battles for season seven were filmed early in the year, about five months into my pregnancy. I had trouble buttoning the bottom two buttons of my jacket, fast-walked instead of ran around Kitchen Stadium, but I thanked the gods of cuisine that I didn't suffer any food aversions or morning sickness. I had visions of filming the big reveal at the top of the show. *And today's secret ingredient IS . . .* The iron cover rises slowly into the rafters, the dry ice rolls out, and I spy a butchered goat or platters of glistening organ meats or tower of cheese that smells like a dirty sweat sock retrieved from the sewer, and I have to run offstage and throw up in a bucket.

When Jennifer was thirty-six weeks along, I went to a food and wine trade show in Puerto Rico. Our doctor assured us that she had a good two weeks to go, easy. I would only be gone four days, and would be back in plenty of time to be there for the birth of our third child. The day I left she decided she wanted to take Zoran and Caje to Disneyland, a last hurrah before the baby arrived. I begged her not to, believing that walking miles around an amusement park on a warm California day while nine months pregnant would induce labor, but she either didn't believe me, or just wanted to do what she wanted to do. When I called to check in from Dallas, where I was catching my connecting flight, I could hear the noise of the park in the background—calliope music, whoops of people having fun, Zoran and Caje chattering at her side.

I made it to San Juan and checked into my hotel room, and at a little after 1:00 a.m., fell into bed. I was still folding and fluffing the too-skinny hotel pillow under my head when the phone rang. Our friend Michelle said, "Hi, Cat," and I started cussing. I knew why she was calling.

Jennifer was in labor.

I was dog tired, pissed off, worried, heart bruised, and did I mention pissed off? Jennifer was an independent woman and could do as she pleased, but I wished she had listened to me. Frantically, I tried to put together a plan. I could check out now, grab a few hours of shut-eye at the airport, and take the first flight out. But it was no use. Even as my brain was racing, I knew I would miss the birth.

I went to sleep, or tried to. In the morning I called and Jen was still in labor. I was relieved. Even if I couldn't be there, at least I wanted to be awake and alert. An hour later, while I was waiting in the greenroom before my first event, my phone rang again, and it was our doctor.

"Hey, Cathy, we're about to have a baby here, are you ready?" she asked.

I plastered my phone against my ear and listened while Jennifer pushed, and our doctor encouraged her and then I heard the tiny wail, and Thatcher Julius Cora came into the world. Jennifer snapped a picture of him immediately and within minutes I was looking at my new son, who was every bit as handsome as his brothers.

Five minutes later they called for me. I sped out on stage, waved hello, and cooked twice as fast as I did during an Iron

Chef battle. I'm sure the audience thought I was on speed, that's how fast and furious I put that demonstration meal together, sweat flying off my forehead, my hands a blur. Afterward I took the customary pictures with a huge grin on my face, zipped through some autograph signing, and was ushered into a waiting car that sped to the airport, where I caught the first flight back. It was worth every penny.

Jennifer's ability to pop out our kids like a human Pez dispenser didn't rub off on me. My contractions started while I was on a conference call on a Friday. We rushed to the hospital, where I made everyone's life miserable that evening, then throughout the longest Saturday in recorded history, and on into Sunday, forty-eight fun-filled hours of breathing through the contractions while trying not to dwell on every pregnant woman's worst nightmare, squeezing out a nice, long poo the moment the baby is born.

When I was still in labor after two full days, to the best that anyone could tell, my body had begun to reject the epidural. It suddenly felt as if ice water was being injected into my spine. This may have been the point I started hollering, "I'm dying, I'm dying!" Shortly after that the doctor, worried that the baby was stuck in the birth canal, ordered a C-section. Had I known this would have been the outcome, I would have made an appointment for the procedure and saved myself two days of wishing I could throw myself under a train.

Nash weighed 7.5 pounds, beautiful to behold, despite the trauma of his birth. He was Jennifer's biological son, and inherited her dark, almond-shaped eyes. He immediately seemed at home in the world, not unduly alarmed by lights and noises, slept well, took to the boob like a champ. Then, after a mere twenty-four hours of perfect bliss, I was propped up on pillows in my hospital room doing what I thought was an expert job of nursing him when Jennifer looked at him, bent down and looked closer, then said, "Oh my God, he's blue."

She called for a nurse, who rushed in and tore Nash from my arms before I could even utter the words "What the hell?" He was raced to the NICU, the Neonatal Intensive Care Unit, where he was placed in an incubator, a hateful cage of Plexiglas where they hooked him up to monitors that could track his cardiac function and stuck a tube up his tiny nose to oxygenate him. The diagnosis that was no real diagnosis: he was having trouble breathing on his own. Over the next ten days there were MRIs, CAT scans, PET scans, and other tests I've since repressed. Everything was inconclusive. The theory was floated by one of the doctors that perhaps he'd just needed a little help getting his lungs up and running after the stress of delivery.

Nash spent ten days in the NICU. Jennifer and I spent every day and evening with him. I breast-fed him, held him, rocked him, sang and talked to him, everything I could think of to assure him that everything would be all right. At night, Jennifer would go home to relieve the friend who was caring for our other three boys. Every night the nurse would tell me that I needed to go home, too, and try to get some sleep. She would remind me that he was being very well cared for. It was agony. The next morning I would be back before dawn.

Eventually they sent us home, with no diagnosis and an apnea monitor. Day and night he wore a belt around his chest that chafed his armpits. The monitor was supposed to measure his chest movement and heart rate. It went off at least three times a day for reasons we could never glean, having nothing to do with his breathing. Whenever the alarm went off, tears started in my eyes. My nerves were raw from worry.

Meanwhile, Jennifer was caring for Thatcher, who was three

months old and still waking up to be fed twice a night. Meanwhile, Caje was two and had just entered the phase of toddlerhood where he liked to open the kitchen cupboards, remove all the pots and pans, then bang them together before hurling them across the kitchen floor. Meanwhile, Zoran was five, the only one not in diapers, and was anxious about starting kindergarten in a few short months. Meanwhile, Everest-size mountains of laundry gathered. Meanwhile, bills piled up on the dining room table, then slid off the table onto the floor. Meanwhile, we all needed to be fed. Somehow I could battle a world-class chef on national television but could barely get it together to mix up some rice cereal and banana for Caje and roast a chicken for the rest of us.

Meanwhile, my work.

Before I got pregnant, I finally went into business with a restaurant group to open my own place. After *Iron Chef* took off I'd been approached by several people, but nothing that seemed like a sure fit. I knew what I wanted: a place where regular people could get great, interesting food. I wanted to build a restaurant that catered to people like my parents, who worked extraordinarily hard their entire lives, who were savvy home cooks, eating well and keeping alive dozens of beloved recipes from their forebears, but rarely went out to eat because they couldn't afford it. When they traveled, the furthest thing from their minds would be to secure a reservation at Barbuto or the Gramercy Tavern—or the equivalent in whatever city they found themselves in—where they would sit among the so-called beautiful people in their hundred-dollar T-shirts picking at their thirty-five-dollar burgers.

In August, a scant month after Nash was born, Kouzzina ("kitchen" in Greek) opened on the boardwalk at Walt Disney World Resort in Orlando. When in my wildest dreams I imagined the locale of my first restaurant, it hadn't been Disney World, but the opportunity was too good to pass up.

In 2008 I'd signed on with Disney to do an On Demand show called *What's Cooking with Cat Cora* and they'd approached me to see if I wanted to partner with them on a restaurant. It was a licensing deal in which they put up the money to build out the space and launch it, while I focused on creating the menu, designing the décor, and building a culture within the staff. For that, I would receive a percentage of the gross profit.

I was on the verge of having four little kids at home; I'd be supporting six people. Opening a restaurant demands a twelve-hour-a-day, seven-day-a-week commitment and a willingness to tolerate a lot of financial risk at the outset. The arrangement with Disney would allow me to spend time with my family while enabling me to do my part to change the landscape of where regular people eat. Theme parks, department store restaurants, and airports typically served food that was limited, fatty, and subpar, and this would allow me to introduce good, healthy food to folks in a beautiful setting.

Everything I was, everything I believed in, went into creating this place. It occupied an existing restaurant space (goodbye, Spoodles), but part of the deal included renovation. I wanted to offer adults and adventurous kids something a little more elevated than the usual club sandwiches, cheeseburgers, and fish-and-chips, in an environment that was restful, or more restful than the usual Disney boardwalk eatery. I wanted to create a place that kept the kids happy, while their parents could enjoy sophisticated wine and food. I wanted to offer a respite from the whimsy, an oasis.

The designers knew it would be Greek influenced, and at first they showed me blue-and-white china and napkins and thought the walls should be plastered with Greek travel posters, the ones we've seen a hundred times before, with a white village perched on the side of a mountain overlooking the bright blue sea.

"That's Greek kitsch," I said. "Too hokey."

I wanted a restaurant that you could airlift into an upscale Manhattan neighborhood. I aimed to evoke elements of Aunt Demetra and Uncle Yiorgios's home in Skopelos, the rustic wooden table beneath the ancient olive trees, laid end to end with platters of bread, hummus, tzatziki, spicy feta spread, artichoke hearts, spanakopita stuffed with fresh spinach, and those wobbly ladder back chairs we'd sit in for hours, eating and talking.

Kouzzina had an open kitchen—shades of Postino—with marble surrounds and big copper pots hanging from the ceiling, gleaming in the fire from the open woodstove. We also put in a walk-up pizza window for folks strolling by on the boardwalk. I knew every parent there needed to fortify the troops before setting off for the day, so we opened for breakfast. Steel-cut cinnamon oatmeal, blueberry orange granola pancakes, Greek yogurt with fresh fruit, and turkey sweet potato hash with two eggs and arugula salad topped that menu. Dinner was trickier. I could now see how easy it was to fall into Giant, Ten-Page Menu Syndrome.

I'd put my name on four wines I'd sourced from Northern California, two red and two white, and also served Mediterranean sangria. The bread service came with olive oil and a few perfect kalamatas. Appetizers included calamari, grape leaves stuffed with a good goat cheese, and that old showstopper, saganaki: fried cheese flambéed at the table to the cry of *opa!* and then extinguished with a squirt of lemon. I had to offer spanakopita and *kota kapama* as entrées, and also a whole fish, even though I suspected we wouldn't move a lot of them. (Too many thoughts of Nemo.) For sides, I offered caramelized Brussels sprouts, salt-roasted beets, and Spiro's Greek salad, named for my dad. My substitute for french fries? Smashed garlic-fried potatoes. Desserts: a dense, dark chocolate budino, a molten chocolate pudding cake, and, of course, baklava.

Kouzzina's grand opening was September 17, a mere two months after Nash was born. He'd been sprung from his apnea monitor by then. His pediatricians thought that whatever had been wrong with him had resolved itself, even as it had come close to putting his mothers in a rubber room. He would live. Indeed, as I write this he is as hardy as a Viking.

But leaving my little guy then was excruciating. I was a wreck as I laundered and packed my chef whites. The way I carried on, you would have thought he'd been ripped from my arms by a cruel despot, never to be seen again. I sobbed as I packed, sobbed in the cab on the way to the airport, sobbed as the plane taxied down the runway. I collected myself only when the flight attendant started giving me the side eye. It had taken everything I had to get on the plane and *go*. The last thing I wanted was to be yanked off by a pair of TSA lackeys. My deep fear was that if I didn't go now, I'd never go, and we'd all wind up living out of a shopping cart in one of Santa Barbara's well-maintained parks.

~~~

My parents and my brothers came to the opening of Kouzzina to offer their congratulations. Mike had found himself at last. After his wrecking business in Little Rock, he'd moved into marine engine mechanics, and was now making an excellent living as an instructor at Marine Mechanics Institute in Orlando. He used to amuse the entire family by taking apart the lawn mower and fixing it in ten minutes flat, and now he'd found a way to put that special genius to good use. He was a master mechanic, a "professor" in pressed khakis and a polo shirt with the school's logo on the pocket. He and his wife, Carrie, live in a nice little house on a canal in Kissimmee. He can hop into his own boat, finally, and go fishing with his kids, my niece Anna, and nephews Nicholas and Andrew.

Over the last decade my relationship with Chris had become strained. He had always been the smartest of the three of us. In high school he tested well and had an aptitude for drawing. There was no doubt that he would end up as an architect or something equally brainy and refined. The summer after high school one of his buddies got him a good job driving a truck for Budweiser. Time passed, and he enjoyed the money and freedom, and soon it seemed a little too late to apply for college, and then he met a girl and got married, and he was thrust into adulthood. He saw me parlay my trade skills into a nice career and resented me for it, I think.

But then Kouzzina opened, and Chris showed up to have a look around. He arrived with his family in tow, his wife, Jennifer Ann, and four kids: Morgan, Lexie, Paxton, and Hallie. He wandered in, inspected the black-and-white pictures of our parents' wedding that I'd hung in the entryway, took in the open kitchen with its gleaming copper pots, the box-beam ceilings, and wooden floors, the whole big, busy, efficiently run enterprise, and just said, "Wow, Cathy. This is great. I'm really impressed."

We were in our mid-forties by then. Whatever rancor had grown up between us had dissipated. His generosity—and the fact that he'd come to the opening to support me—moved me more than I could say.

⁓ nineteen ⁓

When you meet Jennifer, she doesn't really strike you as stubborn. She's a laid-back native Californian. No hostile set of the jaw, no laser-eyed stare. She's got a gift for going with it, hanging out, and being cool. Except when it came to Battle Nanny.

After I was fully back at work at the end of 2009, I begged her to consider hiring a nanny, but she was having none of it. I knew she was a great mom and was an experienced nanny in her own right, but now we had four kids under the age of six. We could almost have fielded a basketball team.

"I *am* a nanny," she'd say. "Or I was. And wasn't that the whole point of my staying home? To take care of our kids?"

"We're in the weeds!" I'd counter. "You're doing a great job, of course you are, but you're only one person. All I'm saying is that you could use a little help. *We* could use a little help. And I just can't go out into the world to support us feeling as if I'm leaving you stranded."

"As long as I'm organized I'm fine," she said.

We had this argument many times. Once, as I recall, she was nursing one baby while changing the diaper of the other.

"This is going to break us," I pleaded.

Finally she gave in and we hired Christiana, a Brazilian woman. To this day I can't figure out whether hiring a nanny was too little, too late, or whether Jennifer "agreed" but harbored more bitterness than I imagined. I thought hiring help would ease the tensions between us, but the only thing that changed was having an extra pair of arms around the house during daylight hours. No small thing when you have four little boys under the age of six, but still.

Some people have expressed surprise that the same thing that happens to hetero couples after a new baby enters the picture happens to same-sex couples. One statistic that doesn't surprise me is that 70 percent of the roughly 50 percent of marriages that end in divorce include those with children under the age of seven. I wish I could report that Jennifer and I were different, that our twenty-first-century, bad-ass approach to conception and childbirth continued on into parenting, but I'm afraid we were no different from everybody else. Jennifer resented me because I got to pack my bag, get on a plane, and go, and I resented her because she got to stay home. She felt stuck and glamorized the fun and freedom of travel, and I felt shackled by the demands of being the breadwinner, forcing myself to smile, nod, and engage with the world when I'd rather be in my sweatpants on the sofa, snuggling up with my babies, reading stories.

If we could have just switched roles for two weeks, we would have appreciated each other. She would have gotten out into the world, felt the freedom of being able to just walk along and swing her arms, to put on a T-shirt unadorned by spit-up on the shoulder or weird stains. She would have also seen that while I had some time to myself on the plane, and late at night in my hotel, the rest of the time I kept a packed schedule, racing from meeting to show to demo, with as many phone calls as possible jammed in between. Always exhausting and only occasionally enjoyable.

After Nash finally settled in we never regained the rhythm of our relationship. We were exhausted, hormonal, and stressed. We were grateful and happy we'd fulfilled our dream of creating a beautiful family, but we were both running on fumes.

I had everything I'd ever dreamed of—an interesting and thriving career in the culinary world, a beautiful wife who was both friend and lover, four healthy children, a house overlooking the ocean in the prettiest city in the nation—and yet I'd never felt so depleted. I beat myself up about it. How could I be so tired when this was surely the happiest time in my life? One night I was in my hotel room, having sought temporary relief in the little bottles found in the minibar, and played a game with myself, trying to think when I'd been this exhausted. I came up blank.

My mission had been to be the best chef, the best restaurateur, the best Iron Chef, the best boss, the best wife, the best mother, the best Cat—and it was killing me. I'd gotten to the place I found myself because I was convinced I was iron, but clearly I wasn't.

I would drink myself into a teary stupor, lie on the bed hugging the pillow as if it were my baby, and cry. At first my milk would leak when I thought about Nash, but then too much time passed when I was unable to feed him and my milk dried up.

Sometimes, if the minibar wasn't as well stocked as I needed it to be, I went down to the hotel bar to hang out with the crew, or if I was filming *Iron Chef*, my sous chefs. One drink became four became five.

In early 2010 I received a phone call from Father Alex Karloutsos, head of the Greek Orthodox Archdiocese of America, asking if I would accept an invitation from the White House. The

President and Mrs. Obama were hosting Greek Prime Minister George Papandreou at a Greek Independence Day celebration, and they were hoping I would be available to cook for a party of 350 dignitaries and guests.

"Of course! Absolutely. Sign me up!" In my memory I was shouting like a demented person. Which I pretty much was by then.

I was given permission to bring Zoran, now almost seven, as my guest. I also brought two Greek American sous chefs from Kouzzina to help prep. I was delirious with gratitude and honor. I got teary-eyed thinking about my grandpa Pete opening his diner in Greenville all those years ago, choosing to call it The Coney Island because it was the most American name he could come up with. I wish I could reach back in time and tell him the news, that his own granddaughter would one day be cooking for the president.

I gave up precious sleep to labor over the perfect menu, which would have to be the Menu of my Life.

Cold Plates
Salt-Roasted Beet Tartar with Skordalia on Crostini

Basque-Rubbed Grilled Chicken Thighs in Lettuce "Gyros" with Sumac Onions and Avocado Tzatziki

Olive Oil Roasted Eggplant with Peppers, Tomatoes, and Capers

White House Arugula, Pomegranate, and Spicy Cashew Salad with Lemon Vinaigrette

Greek Salad with Toasted Garlic, Heirloom Tomatoes, and Banyuls Vinaigrette

Chickpea Fritters with Romesco Sauce and Cornichon

Oysters on Ice with Cucumber Ginger Mignonette with Lime Dust

Hot Station

Toasted Sesame Meatball Skewers (Beef and Pork) with Harissa Yogurt

Fishermen's Stew (Scallops, Shrimp, Clams, Mussels, Fish) with Ouzo Butter

Baby Lamb Chops with Feta Chimichurri Sauce

Crab Cakes with Roasted Garlic Yogurt with Dill Pollen

Mini Pastitsio with Béchamel and Roasted Tomatoes

Crisp Spanakopita "Spring Rolls" in Baked Phyllo, with Herbs, Spinach, and Feta

Black Truffled Orzo with and Spring Herbs

Desserts

Rolled Pistachio Baklava

Loukoumades with Honey Drizzle

Kourabiedes Greek Wedding Cookies

Finikia Honey Glazed Nut Cookies

Mini Chocolate Pudding Cakes with Chantilly and Fresh Berries

The morning of the event I met Cristeta Pasia Comerford, the White House executive chef. She had taken over the job after Walter Scheib, my old *Iron Chef* nemesis, had resigned in 2005. We hit it off immediately. We were both petite women who'd stumbled into first female White House chef and first female Iron Chef respectively. Cristeta also had an Iron Chef battle under her belt. She was paired with Bobby Flay, and they fought Emeril Lagasse and Mario Batali in Battle White House Produce (in which they prevailed, 55–50). She gave me a quick tour of the surprisingly small kitchen she normally worked in, and the bigger navy kitchen where I would be working that day.

I wanted a peek at the famous organic garden, and as a White House page led us outside I heard one of the guards say into his walkie-talkie, "They're going into the garden, have your sniper stand down." Never did I imagine I would have an AK-47 bead on me while I was picking lettuce.

The meal prep was the usual blur. Even at the White House, plating a lamb chop is plating a lamb chop. Afterward, two Secret Service guys, or whom I presumed to be Secret Service guys, rushed my two chefs, Zoran, and me into a back room. They shut all the doors, glanced out the windows. Suddenly, the president and First Lady were there. Zoran reeled back, wide-eyed. They were so tall and beautiful, the president in his perfect dinner jacket, the First Lady in a gold ball gown that made her look like a goddess. We all shook hands. After thanking me for my service, he opined that the grape leaves were superb. She favored the lamb chops.

Perhaps my greatest joy that day was the presence of my parents, whom I was permitted to invite to the reception. The night had been a triple treat for them: as Greek Americans, as the parents of the chef, and as true southern yellow-dog Democrats who'd worked to elect the president.

⁓ twenty ⁓

In 2010, a friend of ours in Santa Barbara introduced us to hot yoga. Every class was ninety minutes long, the same twenty-six postures held for ninety seconds each and repeated twice in a controlled climate of 105 degrees and 40 percent humidity meant, I guess, to make you feel as if you're practicing yoga in India during the monsoon season. Jennifer and I went a few times and it was all right. A little boring for my taste. I felt loose and relaxed after class, if a little stupid from the heat. And this is coming from a girl who survived summers in Mississippi.

Jennifer began going regularly, three times a week. She urged me to join her for classes, but that style of yoga is all-consuming, and demands a degree of dedication I didn't possess. I was now traveling close to two hundred eighty days out of the year, had four children under the age of I can't even remember at this point, and a marriage that needed some TLC. Plus, the pressure to stay in shape and well groomed at all times, in the event a call came from a talk show or I was invited to be a guest judge that would require me to hop on a plane with twenty-four hours' notice and be presentable in HD. Tony Bourdain can travel the world looking haggard and snaggletoothed, Mario Batali can show up in his scuffed clogs and carrying twenty-five extra pounds, and Gordon Ramsey can look wrinkly and exhausted, but female chefs are held to a higher standard. That standard being a starlet on the red carpet. All of which is to say, I could barely squeeze in my own workouts, which were by necessity short and efficient.

But Jennifer loved it. She's always enjoyed yoga, and hot yoga challenged her in a way other classes didn't. For a month or so things between us improved. Before, she'd been reluctant to leave the boys with our nanny, Christiana. I was relieved that she'd found something that gave her a reason to get out of the house, something out in the world that captured her interest. I bowed down before her fierce and competent mothering, but I believed it would be good for her to find something that was hers and hers alone.

After a few months, she began going to class five days a week, then seven. Then twice a day. Her teachers cautioned her to take it easy. Three hours a day of yoga in 105-degree heat could be bad for your health. People regularly passed out from heat exhaustion. Jennifer already had so much on her plate. She ran the household, paid the bills for my business, and took care of our four little boys. I worried that it was too much.

The next time I came home from a business trip, I had no memory of where I'd been—like dinner service and *Iron Chef* battles, all the events, conferences, seminars, festivals, appearances, consultations, panels, and talks were becoming a blur. I returned to find Jennifer sitting on the floor in shorts and a tank, stretching her legs. My heart gave a good thump just seeing her there, I loved her so. She was talking to her mom on the phone, deep in conversation. I took my suitcase into our bedroom, busied myself unpacking until she was finished with her call. I wanted to be with her, to reestablish our connection right that minute.

After she hung up I took her in my arms, suggested we get

e meetings did help to a degree. But my marriage wasn't
nly repaired because I passed up a glass of pinot.
uring those desperate days I also tried to find some heal-
nd strength by spending time enjoying my boys. But I
heir anchor, not the other way around.

ried everything. If someone had told me to go to the
nude and play bongos while praying to the ocean god,
ld have done it.

did do it, sort of.

yogi friend, Rachel, suggested a visit to her father might
order. He was a medical doctor in town, also a shaman
practiced some form of African divination that involved
e readings" in a yurt in his yard. It was legit, insofar as
things are; a tribe in Nigeria that practiced this particu-
rm of healing had ordained him.

crawled inside the yurt and sat cross-legged in front of a
able. He fetched a velvet bag and withdrew a handful of
s, which he tossed across the table, then gazed at, drum-
his chin. He murmured that he saw an intruder. "There
neone or something in your life who is a danger to you.
ething disrupting your marriage and your life."
nodded, wondered how crazy he thought I would be if I
knew exactly what he meant: hot yoga.

⁓

011, I opened a new restaurant, Cat Cora's Kitchen, at
an Francisco International Airport. I'd flown eight hun-
million miles over the past fifteen years, and every time
rched through the terminal in some far-flung airport I
ys thought the same thing: why does airport food have
e so god-awful? It's not as if an airport is the interna-

a sitter, go out alone together to do something, anything. "We haven't been out on a date in months and I've missed you."

She looked at her watch. "Actually, I wanted to hit that evening class. Maybe tomorrow?"

⁓

Jennifer was drifting away, further each day. One day, she asked if we could talk. Oh, honey, yes. Let's talk. Let's get it all out into the open. Anticipating her apology, I was readying my own. I needed to work less, drink less, and be there for her and the boys.

She said she'd been giving it some thought, and decided she wanted to become a hot yoga instructor. I thought that sounded terrific—until she said it would mean leaving for a nine-week intensive course. *Nine weeks away from home?*

We then proceeded to spend many hours and thousands of dollars in the office of the world's most patient couples' counselor, hashing out this single issue. I talked until my throat was as raw as my nerves.

"When the kids are a little bit older you can do this. Just wait a couple years. Hot yoga will still be there!"

Her response? To go home and shave her head.

Actually, that's not quite how it went. I was traveling—again—and she called to tell me that while she understood she was going to be forced to delay her dreams even as I got to live out mine every single day, she wanted to make a change, to do something to feel lighter and freer.

"Go for it," I said. At this point, I was well aware I had to pick my battles. If any woman could pull off the bald look, it was Jennifer. She has a beautiful face and head shape, high supermodel cheekbones. She said she wanted to be free from her hair. I said fine, be free.

Not everyone was so sanguine. A few years earlier I'd hired a manager, William. Right about the time Jennifer shaved her head, *O, The Oprah Magazine* called and said they wanted to do a Cat Cora and family photo spread. They wanted to send a crew to shoot at the house.

"How in the hell are we going to do that when Jennifer just shaved her head and she looks like a cancer patient?" William said. "Do you think she'd wear a wig?"

I laughed until the tears were running down my cheeks. "William, that is a phone call you're going to make. I am not touching that one. You want to call her and invite her to wear a wig for an *Oprah* photo shoot, you go right ahead."

Indeed we appeared in the pages of the magazine as a family in an article entitled *The Family That Eats Together*. Jennifer did not wear a wig.

We limped along for several months, something we could do because when we were at home together there was always someone who needed changing, feeding, rocking, bathing, singing to, playing with. During the few rare moments of inactivity, Jennifer would go to yoga and I would crack open a bottle of wine and get caught up on work. This became our habit. Our connection had withered to the point where the only things we had in common were the kids and the same house key.

Did I blame myself? Yes indeed. I'd known it would be tough, being responsible for the care of four very active, very little boys day in, day out, but I'd tried to make it up to her. I'd gotten a gig doing cooking demos aboard a high-end cruise ship that would enable us to travel. In 2007 we'd traveled, as a family, to Egypt, Jordan, and Mumbai. The next year we went to Easter Island. We spent every Halloween at the Disney Resort in Orlando. One thing I was missing, of course,

was that Jennifer had to have her own li[...] something for herself. My bestowing a [...] tion upon her did nothing to address the [...] something that was just for her.

I did everything I could think of to [...] marriage. Tapped into my spiritual base [...] with Jennifer and without. Prayed my h[...] tried to be more open, less judgmental. [...] to my mom. A lot. Did yoga (not hot yo[...] cised. Drank more wine than I should h[...]

My urge to drink every night bother[...] blacking out or getting smashed, but I di[...] glasses of wine or a cocktail or two befo[...] of wine or two with dinner, every night, [...]

I began attending a twelve-step prog[...] house, a 5:00 p.m. meeting that attracte[...] ished businessmen and businesswomen i[...] dollar shoes to homeless folks who had [...] many days. The diversity appealed to m[...] community, and we were all there to ge[...] kind, whether it was to hear a story you [...] that scared you straight. For some peopl[...] tries were their only meal of the day.

I was still drinking while going to m[...] sounds contradictory, but I wasn't alone [...] was sober, but some were like me, desp[...] urge to drink and self-medicate with enli[...] ready to commit to the twelve steps. I kep[...] ing it would help me slow down, or help [...] four glasses of wine to one nice glass wit[...] would help me learn how to drink occas[...] ing to think about it.

tional space station and transporting good meat and produce required the brightest minds at NASA.

I'd spent so many frantic, excited, depressed, sad, joyful moments in airports, so I understood in my bones that people in transit needed a reprieve, a rest from the lunatic demands of air travel. My idea was to offer upscale comfort food in a restful environment. I put lobster mac 'n' cheese, classic American grilled cheese and tomato soup, and flank steak tacos with charred pineapple salsa on the menu, and an ouzotini on the drinks list. I made sure the bartenders poured real drinks, and had the designers install outlets under the bar, so people could charge up their electronics.

That fall, Jennifer and I had decided we should go to Jackson for Christmas. Earlier in the year my dad had been diagnosed with bladder cancer. He survived his surgery and treatment and had been declared cancer free, but it was clear his best years were behind him, and there was every possibility this would be his last winter holiday.

As Christmas approached, Jennifer said she just didn't want to leave her yoga practice. The argument that ensued was not our worst, in part because the moment I was about to start throwing things, Thatcher toddled out, complaining of a sore throat. The next day the doctor diagnosed strep. Most likely we could have found a way to make the trip, but by then Jennifer had worn me down. Two days before Christmas I called my parents to break the news that we couldn't make it. They were crushed. My mom, steely, practical, and always understanding, cried. It was, indeed, my dad's last Christmas. Even now I prefer not to dwell upon that, for fear of unearthing the resentment I know is buried there.

~ twenty-one ~

My dad was the world's best retiree. After thirty-five years devoted to teaching world history to tenth graders in the Jackson, Mississippi, school system, he said, "No more." They must have given him a plaque and a send-off dinner, but if so I never heard about it. He was the classic Man Who Never Looked Back.

In retirement he would get up at 9:00 a.m. and drink a cup of coffee, eat a toasted bagel heavy with cream cheese, and read the paper. Next: shit, shower, shave. That took two hours. Then he would meet a friend for lunch. One of his students grew up to become principal of the high school, and they'd often go to Scottie's restaurant, now no longer in business. He developed a routine with the waitress. She'd say, "How were those chicken and dumplings?" And he'd say, "Real good. But next time trip the chicken so some meat falls off."

He'd mosey home, settle into his recliner, and read his book. Heat up the leftover coffee from the morning's pot and wait for dinner, wondering in particular what was for dessert. As he got on in years, he developed type 2 diabetes, and my mom begged him to watch his calories and exercise. I had a few come-to-Jesus conversations with him about cutting out the hand pies, but he just smiled, indulging me. "I've already outlived all the men in my family," he said.

After he recovered sufficiently from his bout with bladder cancer, my parents made the long trip from Swan Lake Drive to Santa Barbara to visit their grandchildren for Easter, a compensation for missing Christmas. We were relieved and grateful to learn that his oncologist in Jackson had declared Dad cancer free, but a week into their stay, a golf-ball-size tumor popped up on his neck. Jen and I took him to our doctor, who diagnosed the mass in his lymph nodes as malignant. Whether it was a new cancer or a metastasis was unknown, but we were devastated.

Had this happened today, I'd like to think I would be capable of being present with my grief, but instead I went into full-throttle we-are-going-to-make-the-most-of-every-moment mode.

My dad seemed happiest when he had two grandsons on each knee. He loved them more than anything. And regardless of how tense things were between Jen and me, and how I felt that no matter how hard I was working, I should be working harder, longer, and faster, our boys were a constant source of joy for me as well, affectionate and entertaining and wonderful to behold.

Zoran, our oldest, is a Renaissance guy. He plays chess and the piano. He also surfs. He's a good student and a little soccer star. Of the four boys, in terms of looks and personality, he's Jennifer's mini me, sensitive and passionate. He likes people, and during the many plane flights he's already taken, often strikes up a conversation with his seatmate. Perhaps because he was our first and only child for a few years, Zoran and I have a special, unspoken bond; also, because he and Jennifer are so much alike they squabble, and I'm often the peacekeeper.

Caje, the second oldest, is a smaller guy with a huge personality, like the proverbial big dog in a small dog's body. He entertains the rest of us by walking around the house reciting movie lines. It wouldn't surprise us if he wound up becoming a famous actor. Or a Supreme Court judge. He's the law-and-justice man in the family. If Caje sees what *he* perceives as an injustice, he'll start raising Cain about it. If one of his brothers is getting disciplined and Caje believes it to be unfair, he will stand up for him to the point of getting his *own* time-out.

Thatcher is our third born and resembles Zoran to a scary degree (meaning he also looks just like Jen), with the same handsome, well-proportioned features and sly smile. He's our resident wild man, who hates wearing shoes, shirts, or underwear. He was ahead of the crowd in developing his small motor skills, and he's good with his hands, a Lego-assembling genius. He's also got a big vocabulary, and for this reason is hugely entertaining. He uses his big words to try to reason and negotiate.

Nash, the baby of the family, is only three months younger, and Thatcher relates to him as if he were his twin. If he sees Nash is sad about something he'll try to cheer him up by saying, "But look at it this way!" or, "But look, this is why it's going to be so cool!"

Maybe it's always the role of the youngest, but Nash is a rascal. He's fantastically athletic, took to scooter riding, bike riding, and even surfing like he was born to it. He's the kind of boy who will be attracted to cliff diving as a profession. Like Zoran, he's a whiz at soccer, but he also possesses a huge imagination, and loves to play at sword fighting. (All the boys share a passion for this, and I had to get up to speed on the many types of fake blades.) We keep a well-stocked costume drawer, and some days, when Nash has disappeared into his world, he'll change costumes five times a day.

It was late April when my parents arrived in California to see their beloved grandchildren. I was coming apart. I'd stopped seeing Robin for therapy about six months after I began at Postino and hadn't seen anyone else since. I started seeing a new therapist, Judith. She was soft-spoken and very calm, with reddish-brown hair and a maternal quality to which I responded. As is usually the case with very good therapists, I didn't know much about her. Once she told me she loved to swim. We focused on issues stemming from my childhood abuse, which had been stirred up with the birth of my own children. I was beginning to exhibit signs of PTSD. Nightmares set in the house in Texarkana. Flashbacks to that day in the bathroom, seeing my dad poke his head through the door with that look of disgust, the likes of which I'd never seen before or since.

As our children grew, and Zoran and Caje, the two older boys, were starting to venture out in the world, going to preschool and play dates, I became obsessed with the idea that someone out there was abusing them. I'd begun to suffer panic attacks where I'd break into a sweat and start shaking and crying.

There's no telling what might trigger an attack. One time, one of the little guys was having a bad morning. When I left the house he was sobbing uncontrollably because he didn't like the shorts or socks or something he was wearing. A typical morning, nothing alarming.

But later that day I was driving and suddenly the image of him sobbing in anguish arose in my mind, and before I could remind myself that he'd been having a fit over some wardrobe issue, I connected his pain to my fear of someone hurting him, then hurting any of the boys. The terror bloomed in my mind until I started crying. My heart was pounding so hard, my hands shaking so badly, I was forced to pull over.

During the first or second session with Judith, I mentioned that my parents were going to be in town. She knew I had some unresolved issues with them, how after the abuse had been discovered, it was never spoken of again. She wondered whether they would want to come in for a session.

Since the babies had been born and Jennifer and I hit the skids, I'd called my mom sometimes several times a week, crying, complaining, and asking her advice. From hotel rooms in Chicago, Dallas, Nashville, New York, Seattle, Atlanta, and New Orleans I would call her from my fetal position atop the six-hundred-thread-count duvet. She was fully up to speed on my despairing, self-medicating, minibar-raiding ways; on Jennifer's newfound devotion to yoga and head shaving. She knew about the exhausting arguments, the brutal silence and lazy, contemptuous sniping. She'd listened for hours. And she'd forgiven us for skipping Christmas because she possessed more empathy than a monastery full of monks.

When I asked her if she and Dad were up to joining me in therapy she said yes without a moment's hesitation. She knew that I'd never fully processed the abuse, that so much of my anxiety, my fierce determination to prove myself long after there was nothing left to prove, was born of that trauma. She felt, I think, some guilt. I wasn't the only one who had lived with it for forty years.

My mom and dad sat together on the couch in Judith's office. The room was bright in the afternoon sun, and I noticed, really noticed, maybe for the first time, how they'd aged. I smiled to myself, remembering when I returned from my internships in France, now a little over fifteen years ago, and I'd thought a little graying at the temples and bad posture signified the beginning of old age. They were in their seventies now. My mom was still strong and hardy, with a thick head of cropped, gray-turning-white hair and a confident, white-toothed smile. My dad was stooped, softer, more vulnerable. He'd survived his cancer but it had taken a lot out of him.

Judith thanked them for coming, but her primary role was as witness. We cried easily, all of us. My mom, prepared as always, fished a packet of Kleenex from her purse. They reminded me of a few things: I hadn't known how old AH was, or how aghast and ashamed his parents had been. I told them that it had happened more than once. My dad struggled to explain his own actions, and the sheer effort he made broke my heart.

"I was just shocked," he said, searching for words. "I didn't know what to do. Obviously, I handled it badly."

He was an honest, old-fashioned gentleman, a modest man. He hadn't abandoned me. He was just stunned, and human, and victim of his own temperament, as we all are.

⁓

After we learned that his cancer had returned, something curious happened. Out of the blue, as though summoned by the universe to try to make amends, AH, having heard of my dad's plight, turned up on their doorstep at Swan Lake Drive. My mom offered him some coffee and they sat at the kitchen table with the floral tablecloth. He was a man in his fifties now, with a wife or ex-wife, I can't remember, a whole life lived. He said he was there to check on my dad, but my parents weren't having any polite southern time-passing chit-chat.

They threw down. Reported on the therapy session, told him what a blow to our family his beastly behavior had been, how my life—even though it looked so good from the outside—had been scarred by his abuse. They didn't mince words.

This middle-aged man, who had probably all but forgotten his crimes, apologized so hard he broke a sweat. Claimed he was full of shame and regret. My mom reminded him he easily could have served time.

It didn't matter to me what excuses he had. What touched me and partially healed me was that my parents, without any urging on my part, had called him to task. This couldn't have been easy for them. They are not the kind of people who enjoy confrontations, but they loved me enough to try to make it right.

⟿

On July 9, my parents celebrated their fiftieth wedding anniversary and I was determined to throw them a party they'd never forget. I wanted to have the biggest anniversary party Jackson, Mississippi, had ever seen. I wanted to invite everyone who'd ever been touched by their goodness and grace: my dad's former students and fellow teachers at Wingfield High, college friends from Millsap, and whatever old pals were still around from his days managing the Shamrock Inn. My mom's comrades in nursing, her nursing students, and leagues of grateful patients at the University of Mississippi Medical Center, her professors, advisers, and dorm roommates at the University of Alabama when she was there getting her PhD. All the crazy people who used to show up at our house for Thanksgiving. All my brothers and my friends who used to hang out drinking beer in the game room. The neighbors who put up with the Cora kids water-skiing around Swan Lake, flooding their lakeside lawns with our rooster tails. And, of course, their own tribe of close friends. It should tell you a lot that they had more friends, good friends, than anyone I've ever known.

But my dad made it clear, through my mom, that he didn't want it. He was tired. Or, he knew in his bones it would be his last hurrah, and only wanted to be surrounded by his dearest friends and most cherished family. My mom should have realized something was up when I gave in without a fight.

I had other plans.

"Packages will arrive at the house," I told my mom. "*Do not open anything until the party.*"

The day of the party the neighbors called my mom on her cell phone. The local florist had flowers for Spiro and Virginia Lee Cora, and didn't want to leave them on the front porch in the punishing July heat. I asked the neighbors if they could just take them, and they said they didn't have enough room for six dozen red roses.

Six dozen red roses, sent by Oprah. I had asked her for a signed picture for my parents for their fiftieth, and she'd also thought to send the roses. I was stunned with gratitude. I hadn't known that my mother, my dying father, and I needed such a grand gesture of kindness, but apparently we did, and I will always be grateful to Oprah for knowing just the right thing to do.

Barbra Streisand was one of my mom's favorites; she was just as nice as could be when I called her up and asked her to autograph a picture for my parents.

Steve Azar, a big country singer who hails from my dad's hometown of Greenville, recorded a special version of my dad's favorite song, "Ring of Fire," dedicated to them on their anniversary.

Duff Goldman, host of Food Network's *Ace of Cakes* and also an accomplished illustrator, drew a portrait of my dad and sent it along. *Ace of Cakes* was one of my dad's favorite shows (after mine, he was always careful to say).

The Obamas sent a letter wishing them happy anniversary, ending their message with *We know how important love is.*

Through the Dream Foundation, a charity based in Santa Barbara that "makes dreams come true" for adults facing life-threatening illnesses, I arranged for a phone conversation between my dad and his favorite orator, Garrison Keillor.

At the party, I thought they would perish from shock and delight. I admit it was overkill. I couldn't help myself. I knew I was building some good memories for the hard time to come. I watched my mom squeeze my dad's hand, put her strong arm around his shoulder, kiss his lips. My dad shook his head, smiled, chuckled, teared up with who knows what emotion. He was still my soft-spoken dad to the end.

Every last over-the-top impulse? Totally worth it.

I stayed on in Jackson after my parents' anniversary party to help my mom, canceling every obligation I could without risking a lawsuit due to breach of contract. For three months, I sat at his bedside. I rubbed his feet and hands with lotion, brought him a heated pillow for his neck where the tumor pressed and caused the most pain. I hired a masseuse to come several times a week. He had lost the taste for his beloved hand pies and could eat only a few bites of Popsicle a day.

He was very tired at the end and went to sleep most nights with the sunset, when the smell of warm grass was strongest in the neighborhood and the lightning bugs came out. My mom and I didn't cook much, preferring a local sushi place she'd discovered. Sushi had come to Jackson! Just like Taki had introduced frozen pizza at the Shamrock Inn, all those years ago. As the house got dark my mom would make us a couple of her favorite cocktails, Voodoos, with iced vodka and Crystal Light lemonade.

The most precious moments occurred when he let me trim his hair and beard. We sat talking face-to-face while he let me spruce him up. I knew time was short and I asked him every question I could think of, including whether he was afraid to die.

"Yes," he said, "but I had a dream I was passing, and you know, it was wonderful."

One of the priceless lessons I learned from my father is that when someone is dying, all they want is you. The best thing you can do for them is to be present.

On the last day, which we didn't know was the last day, because it turns out you never really know, my brothers came. We stood around his bed, prayed, and cried. It was just like when we were kids, the five of us in that house on Swan Lake Drive.

My *Iron Chef* days were largely over. The Food Network says once an Iron Chef, always an Iron Chef, but in season nine they'd used me only twice. Our contracts were nonexclusive, so in 2010 I signed on with OWN, Oprah's new cable network, to develop my own show. The Food Network was not pleased and curtailed my airtime. My last battle was against South Carolina chef Robert Carter. Somewhat predictably, our secret ingredient was that most southern of vegetables, okra. My cuisine reigned supreme, with a score of 51–44, and I should have felt a whole lot more triumphant than I did. The show aired on September 4, three days after my father died on September 1, 2011.

⁓

There was no end to work, opportunities coming my way like tennis balls out of a serving machine. I set about opening two more airport restaurants and a gourmet market. I started two food lines, a cookware line, and even a shoe line (who knows better than me what you need in a shoe when you're on your feet all day?). I opened my first international restaurant, in Singapore.

I landed the spot as cohost for a short-lived Bravo reality series, *Around the World in 80 Plates*, a very ambitious, very expensive show produced by Magical Elves, a great and reputable production company run by people I genuinely liked. (After it wasn't renewed we joked that *Around the States in 80 Plates* would have been a more affordable option.)

The show was a hybrid travel show/cooking contest, where the contestants ran literally around the world, from country to country, attempting to "master" a nation's favorite dish (as if you could actually do such a thing in the week we allotted them). My cohost was Curtis Stone, the adorable Australian chef and cooking show gadabout, with whom I'd worked before. In forty-four days we visited ten countries and four continents. It was like *Top Chef* meets *The Amazing Race*.

The offer dropped in my lap at the eleventh hour. I knew in my bones that it wasn't a good time for Jennifer and me to be apart. We'd barely weathered my father's illness and death, and now here I was preparing to go gallivanting around the world. But I was the sole breadwinner, and there was nothing else this promising on the horizon.

Off I went. We traveled with a caravan of nearly one hundred cast and crew. It was a chef's dream tour: the spice markets of Morocco, the spicy curries and breathtaking Buddhist temples of Thailand, the wet markets of Hong Kong, where pretty much any protein with a heartbeat is there squirmy and blinking, waiting for its fate beside a carrot curl and sprig of parsley. Curtis and I couldn't have had more fun, relieved from kitchen duty for once, spending the bulk of our days in hair and makeup, then standing around bantering.

After the final episode wrapped I flew home, arriving at LAX, an hour and a half south of our home in Santa Barbara. I'd expected Jennifer to be there, waiting for me, but instead I had a message on my cell phone. She'd gotten a sitter for the kids and headed up to the Bay Area to visit a friend. My heart sank. I was sure we were over.

<hr/>

Father's Day, June 2012, was my first without a dad to call in the morning, catching him while he's drinking his coffee and reading the paper. I never even considered it a real holiday; it was cooked up only to complement Mother's Day. Still, I felt low.

Jennifer and I were still struggling forward, sick of each other's shit. We decided maybe a nice lunch at Cold Spring Tavern, an old stagecoach stop twenty minutes from Santa Barbara up Highway 154, the San Marcos Pass Road, would be a fun date. The owners have maintained the Old West decor: wood-paneled, red-and-white gingham curtains at the windows, huge stone fireplace, a wagon-wheel chandelier, with music on Sundays.

Throughout our life together, Jennifer has always been the driver. I have an impaired sense of direction, one of those people who gets lost driving home from the grocery store. The arrangement has always worked for us, and so I had a beer or three, a shot of tequila, never thinking that I was going to wind up behind the wheel. Jennifer had even made a point of calling herself designated driver.

On the way home, I received a text from our old friend, wild-haired Alexa, the one who'd witnessed us falling in love at Tahoe during the whiteout blizzard all those years ago, who'd been at our wedding, who'd helped us celebrate our birthdays. She wanted to know how I was holding up on my first Father's Day without my father.

"It's Alexa, just wanting to see how I'm doing," I told Jennifer as I tapped out the return text. "Offering me condolences."

Despite the shared history, Jennifer didn't harbor the same love for Alexa that I did. In fact, she'd grown to actively despise her. Alexa had behaved badly toward Jennifer at my dad's funeral, pulling her aside and telling her she needed to let up on the yoga, treat me better. On the one hand I appreciated her coming to my defense, but on the other, I ultimately stood with my wife, and Alexa's remarks offended Jennifer and hurt her, too. Not cool.

A few weeks earlier, during a therapy session, Jennifer and I had each talked about what we would have to compromise on in order to make the relationship work.

I said no hot yoga, find another kind of yoga, there are dozens of styles out there. Find one that isn't exclusive and cultish, one that contributes to the health of your home life and doesn't alienate you from your family.

Jennifer said no Alexa, find another friend who doesn't put herself between us, there are millions of people out there.

Alexa and I had been friends for many years. I was sad to make this concession, but nevertheless, I agreed. But now here was Alexa texting me.

Jennifer lost it. I lost it. The fight sprang to life like a forest fire in the middle of a drought. The San Marcos Pass is a windy, two-lane road, one of those crazy California highways that twists through a forest, over a high arched bridge, scenic but potentially treacherous. We shouted at each other at the same time, neither one allowing the other to have her say.

In frustration, she reached across the console between us, grabbed my iPhone out of my hand, and threw it out the sunroof. All of a sudden, Alexa didn't matter, our fight didn't matter—all that mattered was that my cell phone was gone. I cranked around just in time to see it land in the underbrush.

"What the hell?" I shouted.

"You don't need to text her," she said.

We got into it: wild-eyed shouting, spit flying. Meanwhile, she's careening down the road, leaving my phone farther and farther behind in the shrubbery. Finally, she couldn't bear it another second and pulled over. By now we were only about five minutes from home.

"Get out of the car," she said.

"I most certainly am not getting out," I said. "This is a busy highway."

"Get. Out. Of. The. Car."

"I'm not getting out of the car."

"Get out!"

"I'm not getting out! Hand me the damn keys."

She handed me the keys, unbuckled her seat belt, threw open the door, leapt out, and started walking.

So there I was. Left with the car, the driver's door hanging open. Left with my phone back in the bushes up in the San Marcos Pass. I was so furious I could feel my heartbeat in my head. My phone! With my life inside it, all my work contacts, important emails, my calendar. I had to get my phone. That's what I had to do.

I scooted over into the driver's seat, put the car into gear. Blame it on the beers and tequila from lunch; blame it on my upset; blame it on my knack for committing the occasional colossal fuck-up, but before I drove back to find my phone I stopped at the closest bar for a drink. Just to collect myself, just to calm myself down. Then I got back into the car.

I came to a light that had just turned yellow. There were two cars in front of me, and the driver of the first car started through the yellow, then thought better of it and slammed on her brakes. The driver in the car in front of me slammed on his brakes. I couldn't stop in time and ran into him. Fender bender.

The driver of the second car got out and came over to my window. He was a well-dressed Indian guy in a pressed shirt and nice slacks. Even with a few beers under my belt I clearly saw his expression shift from irritation to wicked delight. He'd come to collect my insurance information, but then he recognized me. He pulled out his phone and started videotaping.

All right, I thought. This comes with the territory. By then his girlfriend had appeared at his side to take in the show. Cat Cora, caught in the wild! I was polite. I'm a southern girl, even three sheets to the wind. "I'm being videotaped by two nerds," I said with a smile. Okay, a drunken smile. "Who doesn't just want to go have dinner together. Could do something exciting with their lives. Really."

The couple called the police and sold their twenty-seven-second recording to TMZ.

I was arrested with a blood-alcohol limit twice the legal limit in California, and pled no contest. I was sentenced to three years' probation and paid $2,386 in fines.

Not my finest hour.

You're probably wondering about my phone. Jennifer had marched home, hopped into the other car, and sped back to retrieve it.

~ twenty-two ~

Getting that DUI was easily the most shameful moment of my life, but I've come to view it as a gift. It was a wake-up call. I'd needed to face my postpartum depression problems, tease out how much was hormones, how much was basic disposition. I went to a doctor.

They say you start going to meetings either because you made the decision to stop on your own or because you received a nudge from the judge. According to the state of California, and the terms of my probation, I was required to attend at least eight meetings within a certain time frame. I'd been to meetings before, so walking in and taking a seat wasn't hard, but afterward I was required to present my court card to the leader, and every time I felt myself flush with shame and guilt.

I felt like a total loser. I couldn't shake it. I continued going to meetings for four months after the DUI, and then our family took a trip to Italy and I started up with my few glasses of wine with dinner.

The conventional wisdom is that step one is the most difficult step, admitting that I was powerless over alcohol and that my life had become unmanageable, and I know it has been difficult for me. Until you are able to stand up and say "I am an alcoholic," you can't get well.

If only because it would make a neater, simpler story, I

wish I could tell you that I have stood up and shared, and surrendered completely to the process of recovery, but I'd be lying. I've thought long and hard about my relationship with alcohol, have remembered those long-ago days at Hinds Community College where I would get fall-down drunk most nights of the week, and also the days during the beginning of my career, when I would "cleanse" before a shoot, then guzzle martinis afterward, and also, recently, when I tried to soothe my troubled heart and ease the pain of a marriage in crisis by self-medicating with some nice Chardonnay, but I am not ready to surrender. Not yet. Right or wrong, the trauma of my early sexual abuse, the PTSD that resulted from having endured it, my ongoing anxiety that I'm trying to manage without medication, and the ever-present stress of providing for my wife and kids in a complex profession, has led to a habit of using alcohol to help relieve my stress.

The day is coming when this will no longer serve me. Drinking has become like screwing a porcupine—the pain exceeds the pleasure. I'm engaged in an internal struggle, one that is familiar to millions of others: Do I quit alcohol for good because I know I will be free and happy? Do I try just to drink less (and is that even a possibility?), or do I just pray that one day I'll be blessed with an epiphany and stop drinking altogether? As of this writing I'm going to meetings again, working the twelve steps with my sponsor. And, not surprisingly, I am happier.

Whether I continue on my current path, my drinking and driving days are absolutely over. If I could hop into the Wayback Machine, knowing what I know now, I have not a shred of doubt that rather than try to drive after Jennifer got out of the car that day, I would have pulled over and called a cab. The other night I had a nightmare that I was tooling around behind the wheel with a cocktail in my hand, and I woke up in a terrified sweat. I never got behind the wheel with a single drop of alcohol in me after June 17, 2012, and I never will again.

⁓

I've also focused on getting my crazy schedule under control. Over the years I've said yes to everything, always aware that I was responsible for providing for six people, and fearful that if I said no, another opportunity would not come along. I've said yes, even as it took a toll on my family and myself. Now, after a lifetime of working to distance myself from the confused little girl degraded by abuse, working fiercely to show the world that I wasn't trash, but how accomplished I could be, how perfect, how iron, I've learned to let it go a little. "Being you is enough," has become my daily mantra, courtesy of Deepak Chopra. I started taking time to evaluate each and every opportunity that came my way, no longer automatically saying Hell yes! to everything.

In terms of my marriage, I'm reminded of my response to Donna's tantrum over the broken vinaigrette all those years ago. That it was always going to break overnight. That was the nature of vinaigrette. It broke, and in the morning you reseasoned it, remixed it, and fixed it. That's just what my wife and I are doing, day by day.

We have made it to a place where we can laugh, just a little, about the dramatic events of the past few years. As they say, tragedy plus time equals comedy. I told her she was allowed one head shaving in our marriage, and she said I was allowed one DUI. Recently, I got a tattoo to honor the power of forgiveness and the hope I hold for our love. It's from Rumi, the thirteenth-century Persian poet: *Out beyond ideas of wrongdoing and rightdoing there is a field. I will meet you there.*

We're having some friends over to dinner tonight. All the boys are underfoot, and Jennifer is at yoga, but will be home soon. She has finally earned that yoga teaching certificate, not in hot yoga but in a Vinyasa-based style called CorePower, which is more laid-back, in keeping with her essential nature. I'm proud of her and her accomplishments, as both a mom and a yogi.

Zoran, now ten, is helping me make the salad—Greek, of course, with off-the-vine tomatoes, feta, and glossy kalamatas. Caje is arranging crackers on a plate to serve with my roasted eggplant tapenade. Nash and Thatcher are irritating him by eating them as soon as they are perfect.

In teaching my kids about food, I've adopted the ways of my mom. They have to try everything once. I offer them options —"What do you think tonight? Are we going to have chicken or are we going to have salmon?"—and once we've decided, that's what's for dinner. Like any children, they'd live on pizza and burritos if you'd let them, but they also love artichokes, asparagus, and pork tenderloin. I'm proud of them, too. I think, no matter what else I've done in this lifetime, what mistakes I've made, what times I've let the devil on my shoulder lead me, even what good things I've achieved, these kids are the very best I've done. I got them completely right.

What's on the menu? Oh, I think you know. My *kapama*, still and always my favorite dish. I pat the chicken dry with paper towels, mix the cinnamon, salt, and pepper in a bowl, and rub the chicken with it on all sides. Mince some garlic. Heat up the olive oil. I put my head down and as the Greeks say, *siga, siga*, slowly, slowly, I begin to cook.

∼ Acknowledgments ∼

Thank you to my incredibly gifted writer, Karen Karbo. Thank you for nourishing my stories with the ultimate deference and care, for hearing my life without judgment but with empathy over many great tuna-jalapeño melts. You got it just right.

To my mom, Virginia: you are always a beacon of light in my life. I am eternally grateful that you adopted me and made me always feel safe, loved, and chosen. I love you, Mo. To my father, Spiro, who I am sure is bragging to God right now about "his girl": I miss you every day, Daddy. To Joanne: thank you for caring for me for nine months, giving me life, and then searching for twenty-one years. You never gave up on me. I love you.

To my grandmother Alma: you continue to be my angel and watch over me; these last couple of years I could have used you a little more, but I know you are there. To Randy and Carla: thank you for always being there for me and our family; you are my parents, too. To my brothers, Mike and Chris: my love and respect is immense. Jeff, Carrie, Jennifer Ann, Jason, Kim, and Michelle: I am so proud you are my brothers and sisters. To my awesome nieces and nephews, Morgan, Nicholas, Alexi, Anna, Andrew, Paxton, and Hallie: dream the biggest dreams, because you can—you will—make them happen, end of story. To my godparents, Taki and Maria: you have

Acknowledgments

always loved me unconditionally and inspired me to go out into the world.

To my extended family and friends everywhere—you know who you are: thank you for your love and your support.

Thank you to Shannon Welch, my superb, brilliant editor, for believing that my life was interesting enough to fill a book, and for creating a book I can really be proud of. Many thanks to you and the entire team at Scribner!

To Jan Miller and Nena Dupree, my book agents at Dupree Miller: thank you for all the pep talks and encouragement, and for all of your tireless work and dedication.

To Tyler Goff, my talented plate-juggling assistant: thank you for the ridiculously great work you do every day on my behalf.

To Barbara Karrol: thank you for your brilliant counsel, continuing friendship, and, last, your endurance.

Thank you to all my business partners at HBF, Hojeij Branded Foods. I want to extend a special thanks to Regynald G. Washington, the CEO of my fan club, for your belief in my talent over the years. Thank you to my teams at the Cat Cora's Kitchen and Cat Cora's Gourmet Market airport restaurants at San Francisco International, Houston, Salt Lake City, and, as of this writing, Atlanta, as well as my international partners and team at Ocean by Cat Cora on Sentosa Island, Singapore, and Resorts World Sentosa (RWS). Thank you all for creating hugely successful restaurants with me and for being the day-to-day supreme teams!

To my partners at Grecian Delight: thank you for your dedication to quality and loyalty.

I want to thank my partners Sherry Villanueva and Brian Kelly at Bird Dog Mercantile in Santa Barbara, and our rocking team at BDM!

Acknowledgments

I want to thank my legal teams at Barnes and Thornburg and Manatt, and thanks also to my teams at UTA, 3Arts, and ID PR.

To any other subjects of this book who were at one time either hurt by me or who hurt me, I give the gift of this quotation:

> As I walked out the door toward the gate that would lead to my freedom, I knew if I didn't leave my bitterness and anger behind, I'd still be in prison.
>
> —Nelson Mandela

I am free.